Lose Weight
Burn Fat
Tone Muscle

Easy 3-step guide for women
to create a lean, strong,
and healthy body

Susan Mascarenhas

Published in 2021 by Independent Publishing Network

Copyright © Susan Mascarenhas 2021

All rights reserved. No part of this publication may be reproduced, stored in a retrieval system, or transmitted in any form or by any means, electronic, mechanical, photocopying, recording, or otherwise, without the prior permission of the copyright owner.

The information in this book is intended to be used for educational purposes only and is not rendering medical, healthcare, or other professional advice. Please consult your GP before embarking on any diet or exercise program. The author claims no responsibility for any liability arising directly or indirectly as a result of the use, application, or interpretation of the material in this book.

ISBN:9781800683600

Table of Contents

INTRODUCTION 5

NUTRITION – 80% of the equation 9

    Why dieting doesn't work 9

    What is intermittent fasting? 16

    Intermittent fasting: find the right method for you 23

    The importance of the right nutrition 30

    How much should I eat? 40

    Creating your meal plan 45

    Starting out 47

    Stepping it up a notch 54

    How to break a plateau 57

    How to increase your protein intake 60

EXERCISE – 20% of the equation 65

    Why long cardio sessions don't work 65

    Burn fat in 10-minute cardio sessions 66

    Strength and resistance exercises 70

    Creating your exercise plan 91

    Starting out 92

    Stepping it up a notch 94

YOU – Getting across the finish line 97

CLOSING WORDS 113

REFERENCES 115

INTRODUCTION

We all want to look good and feel amazing. It should be simple, right?

Then why is it such hard work?

Because we are going about it the wrong way.

We all have different goals. For some, it might be to lose that extra weight or shift that stubborn belly fat. For others, it might be finding a way to eat more healthily without altogether banishing those foods you love. And for some, it may be wanting to gain more energy and wake up feeling vibrant.

Whatever your reason, when it comes to living a healthier lifestyle, the objective should be to feel your best every day - without it feeling like a chore.

You are not alone if you are dissatisfied because you have tried all the diets, pills, and various concoctions available out there to lose weight and look younger. It's not surprising we diet. A multi-billion weight loss industry has been pushing temporary, quick-fix diets on us for years. One problem with these diets is: if you can't enjoy it, you can't sustain it. And if that's the case, they won't work. Even if you manage to 'go on' a diet and lose some weight, what happens when you 'come off' that same diet?

And it's not just that these diets are unsustainable. They do more harm than good to our bodies. They slow down our metabolism, create high spikes in all the wrong hormones, and decrease the levels of hormones we want more of, so when we return to regular eating patterns, the weight piles back on again – sometimes even more than before.

If you feel you are fighting a losing battle to achieve a healthy weight, you are not. We have a great deal of control over our hormones and metabolism. If we eat well, exercise right, and manage stress, they will respond, and I want to show you how.

I am not a personal trainer or nutritionist; all my knowledge of nutrition and exercise has been purely self-taught over the past two decades. However, I am so passionate about it, and I want to help you achieve the body you want.

This book will help you **transform** your body in three simple steps:

Step one: Nutrition

This part of the book will explain why calorie-restricted diets and banishing carbs from your life do not work for your body. It will walk you through intermittent fasting and its benefits, how to pick the method that will suit your needs, the importance of the right nutrition, and how to create your eating plan.

By the end of this section, you will know how to realign your hormones, fire up your metabolism, and eat the foods you enjoy – all while healthily losing weight.

Step two: Exercise

This section will explain why long, drawn-out cardio sessions do not work - and how 10-minute sessions can burn off fat. It will also walk you through numerous strength and resistance exercises – all of which can be done at home - and how to create your exercise plan. And don't worry, you won't be exercising for countless hours to achieve that toned body.

By the end of this part of the book, you will know how to exercise in the minimum of time – while creating toned, lean muscles you are proud of.

Step three: You

Sometimes, just having the right tools and information isn't enough to set us on our journey. This section provides some tips and tools to get you across the finish line.

By the end of this book, you will have all the tools you need to get a leaner, stronger, healthier body and feel more energised.

Make that commitment now to get the body you've always wanted.

Let's get started!

NUTRITION
80% of the equation

Why dieting doesn't work
Dieting may result in a short-term weight loss, but, as is commonly found, these results are usually only temporary. Dieters tend to find they typically regain the weight, sometimes even more, that they had worked so hard to lose.

Why does this happen?

It's not a lack of willpower that makes it difficult to lose weight and keep it off. It's not greed or laziness. Instead, it's your body initiating powerful mechanisms to adjust your hormones and metabolism, to try to regain all the weight you've lost.

Let's look at each of these in turn.

Dieting slows down our metabolism

When we diet or reduce our food intake, our metabolism slows down. Unfortunately, a slow metabolism works against our efforts to lose weight.

Between 60% - 75% of our daily calorie requirements are needed to support processes just to keep our bodies functioning – even when we are fast asleep. These processes include keeping our hearts beating, organs functioning, blood circulating our body, and brains functioning. So, our bodies are working exceptionally hard all the time.

Add to that the energy required for all our daily activities, digesting our meals, supporting our immune system, continuously developing and healing our bodies, and that's a high energy requirement.

Something has to give when we aren't eating enough food to provide our bodies enough energy to fuel these tasks. If this happens, the body begins to prioritize: what roles can it stop spending energy on if they aren't vital to our survival? And so, our metabolism slows.

Some warning signs of a slow metabolism include:
- Unexpected weight gain
- Difficulty losing weight
- Tiredness and exhaustion
- Sugar cravings
- Hair loss, dry skin, and brittle nails
- A decrease in sex drive
- Difficulty concentrating
- In women, menstruation ends or becomes irregular.

All of this takes place because our bodies are striving to save energy for essential processes.

Although our body will turn to our own stored energy reserves, not all of it is from the fat stores we want to deplete: it turns to our muscles too. We don't want to lose muscle mass as decreasing muscle mass slows our metabolism even more.

The body then adapts further still: it becomes more efficient with its use of energy. A study [1] measured participants of the TV show The Biggest Loser after the show and six years later. Six years later, the participants had regained the weight they had lost, but the study showed their bodies had also adapted to a lower metabolic rate. This lower metabolic rate explains why there is a rapid weight gain when regular eating patterns resume and make it challenging to maintain a healthy weight over time.

Fortunately, we can do something to reverse the slowed-down metabolism, which we will look at in the following pages.

Dieting causes hormonal imbalances
Research at Stanford University found the levels of three essential hormones determine our ability to lose weight. These hormones are leptin, ghrelin, and cortisol. Furthermore, the study showed it wasn't just the levels of these hormones but the timing of these dips and rises which determine how quickly and how easily we lose weight.

Ghrelin
Have you ever wondered what causes you to feel hungry?

Feeling hungry is controlled by a hormone called ghrelin, produced in your stomach. When you are full, your ghrelin levels will be lower, and when your body thinks it's time you should eat, your ghrelin levels will surge, sending signals to the brain that causes you to feel hungry. This process is a natural response by your body, which tries to protect you from starvation.

If you are consistently restricting calories, ghrelin levels in your body are elevated [2], which is one reason why dieting makes people feel hungry most of the time.

A sustained increase in ghrelin levels harms your metabolism: it slows it down, and at the same time, increases the potential for fat storage.

Leptin

Leptin is a hormone produced by your fat cells and works in tandem with ghrelin. While ghrelin is your 'hunger' hormone, Leptin is your 'fullness' hormone. When you have enough fat stored, leptin signals to the body you don't need to eat, and it's safe to burn calories at a regular rate.

However, when you lose weight, your leptin levels drop. When leptin levels fall, ghrelin levels rise, which signals to the body that you need to eat, and in a bid to conserve energy, your body also slows down your metabolism.

Slow metabolism is one of the main reasons why so many people lose a significant amount of weight only to gain it back shortly after.

Cortisol

Cortisol is probably most commonly known as the 'stress' hormone because of its connection to the stress response. However, cortisol is an important hormone that has many functions. For example, it can help control blood sugar levels, regulate metabolism, and help reduce inflammation. It also helps control blood pressure, as well as help the body respond to stress or danger.

However, elevated and prolonged stress can increase cortisol to unhealthy levels.

Adhering to strict diets is stressful. A study looked at the behaviours that accompanied dieting: carefully monitoring one's calorie intake and actual restriction of one's calorie intake, and measured both the psychological and biological stress indicators.
The study concluded that both cortisol production and psychological stress levels were both increased. These two factors are known to cause weight gain.

A study conducted by Yale [3] went even further. It found high cortisol levels encourage the body to store more visceral fat (the deep abdominal fat stored around your organs). And having more visceral fat increases the amount of cortisol secreted by your body in stressful situations, so it becomes a vicious cycle. As a result, the body stores even more fat, and it becomes increasingly harder to lose weight.

The great news is, we can do something about these hormonal imbalances.

Ghrelin and leptin can be controlled naturally, mainly through making smart dietary choices and exercising in the right way - and you will learn precisely how to do both in this book. In addition, getting enough sleep and managing stress levels can help you maintain healthy cortisol levels. We will take a look at how to do this too.

We become preoccupied with dieting
Diets keep us so preoccupied with our weight that we stop listening to our intuition, hunger, and bodies for what we need.

When we become preoccupied with pounds lost or gained, we lose sight of our body composition, which is a far better indicator of health. You may have heard of the term 'skinny fat': slim people with a higher percentage of body fat and a low level of muscle mass than is deemed healthy.

Instead of using the bathroom scale to measure our success (or not), it would be better to follow a nutritious plan and focus on how we feel. So, stop focussing on the number and start making yourself the priority.

Dieting can be inconvenient and unsocial
If you are on a restrictive diet, you may find yourself having to eat different meals from the rest of the family. Or you may feel you aren't able to go out for dinner or fully enjoy family celebrations. It takes away the true joy and pleasure of eating and socialising. And really, how sustainable is living your life this way?

We fall off the wagon
Dieting affects our connection with food: have you ever been on a strict diet for a while, but then you 'fall off the wagon' and find yourself in the kitchen looking for something – or anything - to eat because you are just too hungry?

Or perhaps you've decided you will never eat a particular food again – say chocolate, and then find you have developed the biggest craving for it? Then, despite your best efforts, you somehow snap, give in, and before you know it, you have consumed an entire family-size bar?

Denying yourself the foods you love bestows on them a unique and powerful status in your mind that they don't deserve.

You may blame it on greed or a lack of willpower, but actually, it's your body responding to perform its critical functions and stay healthy. When you don't eat enough, your body craves energy because it's in a negative energy balance. When we run out of fuel, hormones get triggered to prompt us to eat. As a result, we become ravenous, which can lead to binge eating or eating past fullness. Then? The guilt sets in, and we are off on the strict diet rollercoaster again.

It is easy to become obsessed with foods perceived as 'bad', and develop unhealthy guilt when eating the 'wrong' foods. To the extreme, it can increase the likelihood of developing eating disorders.

Instead, we need to improve our relationship with food, provide our bodies with the necessary nutrition to function effectively, and allow ourselves to enjoy the foods we love.

Dieting, perceived as the solution by many, is the problem. Continuing on this path damages our physical and mental health and makes us feel inadequate and miserable, and it doesn't do much for our self-worth and self-esteem.

The weight fluctuations that occur from being on and off diets in a repetitive cycle are potentially more dangerous to our health and wellbeing than not dieting at all. There are also the psychological and emotional factors of being on that roller coaster and feeling defeated.

Now we can see how dieting doesn't work; what do we do?

We can take back control and address the underlying cause of weight gain and lingering body fat. We realign our hormones and reset our metabolism. Even if you are at your target weight, perhaps you feel you too need a reset?

How good will you feel, putting in place a proven plan to eat well <u>and</u> achieve the body you want?

It's entirely under your control in the next section.

What is intermittent fasting?

Intermittent fasting is based on <u>when</u> you eat rather than <u>what</u> you eat. Therefore, you will be eating during a set time, and you will be refraining from food for another set time. These times are often referred to as your eating window and fasting window.

With intermittent fasting, no food groups are eliminated or banned. Not only is that great news for our enjoyment and satisfaction – but it is critical for our bodies. You will soon discover why this is. So, you really will be able to enjoy all your favourite foods, without feeling guilty!

There are many different ways we can implement intermittent fasting. We will cover three of the most popular and successful in the next section, together with the pros and cons of each one, and which one might be better suited to you, based on your current priorities and goals.

Intermittent fasting is easier than you might think. We already fast every day – we fast while we're asleep. Intermittent fasting can be as simple as extending this fasting period a little longer by having a later breakfast.

Our bodies are equipped to go without food for several hours and even days; this is how humans survived - and thrived - when they were hunter/gatherers. Obesity, diabetes, and premature aging were not issues that our forefathers faced; they are relatively new to the modern world.

We don't even need to go that far back in time. Looking back just 50 years ago, before video games, an abundance of food, and 'a world that never sleeps', we were more active and ate less.

When we are constantly eating, we are not giving our body a chance to burn its fat stores. Add to this our increased levels of inactivity, and our body isn't even burning the calories we are consuming multiple times a day. As a result, large fat stores put us at risk of obesity, heart disease, diabetes, and other illnesses.

By practicing intermittent fasting, we allow our bodies to start burning their fat stores once they have used up all the calories they received from your last meal.

Given how excess weight on the body significantly contributes to health problems, you'll discover that intermittent fasting will allow you to gain far more than your target weight. It will also keep your body healthy for longer, slow down the aging process, and help you achieve a better body composition: less wobble, more tone.

The benefits of intermittent fasting
1. Weight loss
Many people are attracted to intermittent fasting to lose weight.
There are three key reasons behind the weight loss results.

Firstly, intermittent fasting causes you to eat fewer meals in general, as you're eating within a shorter time frame. So as long as you are not eating significantly more during this eating window, you'll consume fewer calories.

Secondly, in between eating meals, our insulin goes down as the body depletes its glucose stores. Low levels of insulin allow our body to tap into our fat stores to use for energy. Intermittent fasting allows our insulin levels to lower, and for long enough, for your body to be able to burn off significant stores of fat.

Thirdly, the pattern of eating during specific times and fasting at other times speed up your metabolism. One study [4] found that fasting can increase your metabolism by up to 14%. Experts believe fasting helps support the part of the brain responsible for specific metabolic processes (the hypothalamus nuclei) as it is responsive to ghrelin, leptin, and insulin levels.

A study over 24 weeks showed a weight loss of up to 8% with intermittent fasting. The study also measured waist circumference: participants demonstrated a loss of between 4 - 7%. This loss is of particular importance, as it indicates that this was a loss of visceral fat.

Visceral fat is more harmful than subcutaneous body fat (the fat you can pinch), as it lays deep within the abdominal cavity, and is stored around your organs, including the liver, kidneys, and pancreas. It can lead to heart disease, dementia, and cancer.

The good news is visceral fat is usually the first fat to be used by the body, and one of the best ways to lose visceral fat is to increase the amount of protein you consume. We will cover protein intake later

2. Helps reduce insulin resistance

Insulin is a hormone made in your pancreas, and it has two main functions.

Firstly, insulin enables the cells throughout your body to absorb glucose for energy to perform their functions. Glucose is created from the food you eat when it's broken down in the digestive tract.

Secondly, insulin helps regulate your blood glucose (blood sugar) levels. When too much glucose is in your bloodstream, insulin signals your body to store excess glucose in your liver or body fat. The stored glucose is only released when your blood sugar levels decrease, for example, in between meals or when your body needs that extra burst of energy.

Insulin resistance happens when the cells in your body do not respond to insulin appropriately. This prevents the cells from being able to absorb glucose from the bloodstream. As a result, your pancreas creates even more insulin to assist the glucose absorption into your cells. However, if the pancreas cannot produce enough insulin to absorb glucose from the bloodstream, blood sugar levels remain high. Insulin resistance is associated with pre-diabetes and type 2 diabetes.

Insulin resistance can be caused by several factors, including genetics, obesity, aging, and a low level of physical activity.

Although some factors such as family history and age are unchangeable, we can alter lifestyle risk factors such as diet, physical activity, and weight.

Intermittent fasting can significantly decrease blood sugar levels, which helps reduce insulin resistance [5] lowering your risk of type 2 diabetes.

3. Increases human growth hormone (HGH)

The human growth hormone is a hormone produced naturally by your body, in the pituitary gland, located at the base of the brain. It plays a vital role in cell regeneration, tissue repair, and ensuring the healthy growth of muscles and bones.

We produce this hormone throughout our lives, but as we age, levels decline. For men, this decline starts at around the age of 35. In women, the decline begins as early as their 20's. Some signs of declining HGH levels include thinning hair, dry skin, increased belly fat, and the onset of wrinkles.

HGH injections have been used to enhance performance in athletes, and their use in sport was banned in 1989 by the International Olympic Committee's medical commission. However, it's currently being explored for its anti-aging and weight loss properties.

Without going to the extreme of injections, how can we increase our ever-declining levels of HGH?

Research has found HGH increased substantially during fasting periods.

While we are eating, insulin is released in the body, and HGH is inhibited. With fasting, your body can keep insulin levels lower for longer, allowing HGH levels to be higher for longer.

Some foods can naturally enhance your levels of HGH, which we cover later.

4. Slows down the aging process

Factors such as pollution, smoking, pesticides, and a poor diet present our body with oxidative stressors, creating free radicals in our body. Free radicals damage healthy cells causing us to age faster.

Intermittent fasting increases the antioxidant capacity of our body, allowing us to become more resilient to oxidative stress and slow down the aging process.

5. Assists the body in cellular repair

Autophagy, which means 'self-eating', is a process that occurs naturally in our bodies.

Autophagy is a process in which little "hunter" particles travel around your body, hunting for old and damaged cells or cell components. The hunter particles then dismantle these cell components, removing the damaged parts while conserving the valuable bits for subsequent use in creating new cells. These hunter cells can also generate energy for the body by repurposing usable leftover pieces.

Autophagy also defends the body from sickness and infections. Pathogens are bacteria or viruses that, if not correctly dispelled, can invade our bodies and cells. Autophagy kills contaminated cells before they can spread, supporting our immune system.

It also helps our bodies perform effectively because getting rid of waste and damaged portions that are no longer helpful is crucial. If we can't get rid of damaged or broken cells, they'll build up and eventually make us sick. So everything our body does is very efficient, and waste disposal is no exception.

However, our modern lifestyle of 3 meals a day, snacks in between, sugar and highly processed food, together with everyday stress and chemicals in our environment, slow down and sometimes inhibit this natural process.

A study [6] indicated that fasting is one of the most effective ways to stimulate autophagy.

Increased autophagy is also associated with a lower risk of cancer and neurological diseases such as Alzheimer's.

6. Helps reduce unhealthy inflammation
Inflammation is one way the body fights infection. However, too much inflammation in our body can lead to various conditions, such as diabetes, multiple sclerosis, and inflammatory bowel syndrome (IBS).

In recent studies [6,7] intermittent fasting reduced unhealthy inflammation by reducing monocytes, the cells that cause the inflammation, to normal levels.

7. Improves heart health
Heart disease is one of the biggest causes of death in the world today.

There are various health markers associated with heart health and the risk of heart disease: blood sugar levels and inflammatory markers are two of them. We have already seen the positive impact fasting for brief periods has on blood sugar levels and inflammation.

Other health markers are cholesterol and triglycerides. High cholesterol may increase your risk of heart disease, while high triglycerides could lead to the arteries' hardening or thickening of the artery walls, which may increase your risk of heart disease and stroke.

Research has shown that intermittent fasting lowers total cholesterol, LDL (bad cholesterol), and triglycerides and can increase HDL levels (good cholesterol), protecting your heart and blood vessels.

8. Potential to protect against cognitive and age-related diseases
Alzheimer's disease is one of the most common neurological diseases in the world. Because there is currently no cure for Alzheimer's disease, it is critical to prevent it from forming in the first place.

Intermittent fasting studies [6,7] conducted on animals have demonstrated brain inflammation reduction and provided strong evidence that intermittent fasting can delay the onset and progression of Alzheimer's and Parkinson's disease.

Research is currently underway to study the effect on humans.

Intermittent fasting: find the right method for you

As mentioned earlier, one of the great things about intermittent fasting is that there are many ways you can implement it, so you can adopt the method that works best with your preferences and lifestyle.

Below are the three most popular and successful intermittent fasting methods. Let's look at these three, how to implement them, and the pros and cons of each one, which will help you choose which one will work best for you.

The 14:10 method is my preference, as I am fairly active, so I like to support my body with regular meals every day, and I also work better with a set routine.

Pick the one that works specifically to meet your needs and lifestyle. By choosing the method that works best for you, you are far more likely to stick to it and achieve your goals. As we saw earlier, sustainability is a primary key to success, which is why traditional dieting doesn't work.

We'll then move on to discuss the importance of nutrition and how to plan your meals.

If you need some help choosing, my advice would be the 14:10 method.
However, if you aren't currently exercising at all, have a lot of weight to lose, and want to prioritise losing weight first, the 5:2 or Eat Stop Eat options might work better for you. These methods will enable you to lose weight more quickly while you are not dependent on a more regular calorie intake to support exercising.

Once you are more comfortable with your weight, I recommend swap to the 14:10 method and start exercising. Doing this will help you achieve a more toned and shapely body while also ensuring your body has the appropriate calories and nutrients to support this.

The reason for this recommendation is that introducing too much change at once may be hard to sustain, and we want to ensure you achieve your goal. As your diet accounts for 80% of your body, let's focus on that first. Once you begin to see results with your weight, you will feel more inclined and encouraged to add exercise to your routine.

So, focus on the prize, and take one step at a time.

The three most popular methods of intermittent fasting

1. 16:8 intermittent fasting (*14:10 for women)

When you are exercising regularly, this is the best option.

The 16:8 method, popularized by fitness expert Martin Berkhan, is also known as the Leangains method.

*Mark Berkhan's recommendation for women is to implement a 14:10 protocol – eating during a 10-hour window and fasting for 14 hours. This is due to differences in body weight, body composition, calorie needs, and hormones between men and women.

The 14:10 method is one of the most popular styles of intermittent fasting as it is an easy, convenient and sustainable method – implementing this method can be as easy as not eating anything after your evening meal and having a late breakfast.

For example, if you finish your dinner at 8 pm and don't eat until 10 am the next day, you have successfully fasted for 14 hours. This timing works well for people with busy mornings, as it gives you one less thing to worry about – what to have for breakfast. Also, if you are working or active in the morning, you will be more easily distracted away from eating.

Alternatively, if you wake up hungry and like to eat breakfast straight away, you can set your eating window to, for example, 7 am to 5 pm.

Whatever times you choose to set as your eating and fasting windows, it is best to stick to these exact times every day for optimum results. It also helps your body adjust to your new routine.

Pros:
- The 14:10 (or 16:8 for men) method is great for people who often skip breakfast, as it will be the easiest to implement.
- It is very adaptable as your goals and dietary needs change. For example, when you have reached your target weight, it is easy to up your caloric intake to maintenance level (we cover this later) within a 10-hour eating window while still reaping the benefits of intermittent fasting.
- If you exercise daily, this is an excellent method to ensure you are fuelling your body appropriately.
- Most people find this the easiest to establish as part of a daily routine.
- Unlike other protocols, you are regularly eating every day.

Cons:
- For those unable to skip breakfast and who therefore prefer to start their eating window early in the morning, this method may be pretty unsocial:

For example, enjoying family dinners and other evening get-togethers will not be possible if your fasting window begins at 5 pm.

2. The 5:2 diet

The 5:2 diet, popularised by Dr. Michael Mosley, a British television journalist, and former medical doctor, is built on the concept of restricting calories for two days a week and eating normally on the other five days. Calorie intake is limited to 500 calories for women and 600 calories for men on restricted days.

Avoid fasting on two consecutive days; instead, try to balance the fast days in your week, for example, fast on Mondays and Thursdays. Whichever days you choose to fast, keep a minimum of one non-fasting day between them.

There is no rule for when to eat on restricted calorie days. For some people, starting the day with a small breakfast works best, while for others delaying eating as long as possible and then consuming all allowed calories in one meal is the preferred option. Experiment with timing, and see what works best for you.

When you are on a calorie-restrictive day, making every calorie work for you is very important. Choose nutrient-dense foods that will keep you fuller for longer. Meals that are high in protein and fibre will fill you up without consuming too many calories. Lean proteins such as chicken breast and turkey and vegetables are good options. Although pre-prepared calorie-counted ready meals may look like an easy option, these will not be as filling or nutritious.

Although no food groups are excluded on your non-fast days, make sure your diet provides you with all the nutrients your body needs by eating lean proteins, fruit, veg, and whole grains. These food choices will also help you feel more satiated.

Pros
- You can adapt your fasting days to work around social events or family gatherings.
- No food groups are off-limits on your regular eating days; it will help you feel less deprived on your fasting days.

Cons
- Initially, it may not be easy to shift from regular eating to 500 or 600 calorie-restricted days. However, this does get easier over time.
- Restricting calories may present the risk of overeating on your non-restrictive days. If this happens, not only will you not feel great, but you may also sabotage your health and weight loss goals.
- It won't be easy to exercise on fast days with such a low-calorie intake.

3. Eat Stop Eat

The Eat Stop Eat diet, created by Brad Pillon, a nutrition and fitness expert, requires fasting for 24 hours – but you only do this once or twice a week.

Although you are fasting for 24 hours, there will not be a day of the week where you are not eating at all. So, if you finish your last meal at 8 pm on a regular eating day, you will eat again at 8 pm the next day. That counts as a 24 hour fast. Similarly, if you can't start the day without your breakfast and eat that at 7 am, your next meal will be the next day at 7 am.

Pros
- It is more beneficial for people who want to lose weight but want more flexibility in their diet to eat more of their favourite foods.
- The Eat Stop Eat diet is very convenient and flexible to adapt to and change when needed.
- Fasting for 24 hours twice a week will create a huge calorie deficit. For example, if your typical daily calorie consumption is 2,000 calories, fasting for two 24-hour periods will create a 4,000-calorie deficit in a week.
- You are not fasting every day, as in the 16:8 diet.

Cons
- As you fast once or twice a week, it is difficult for your body to become accustomed to your new eating style. As a result, hunger pangs, headaches, and other effects of not eating for 24 hours become a regular feature on your fast days.
- There is a risk of overeating after going through a 24 hour fast.
- Eat Stop Eat is focused mainly on not eating for 24 hours rather than food choices. However, too many unhealthy food choices could sabotage the benefits of the fast.

There are other ways to implement intermittent fasting. However, the above are the most popular, and more importantly, most sustainable. The methods above also make it possible to sustain your body in a nutritional, healthy way.

Other ways to implement intermittent fasting include the One Meal a Day (OMAD) diet and the Warrior Diet. Both encourage eating one meal a day - every day. However, limiting your calorie intake to just one meal a day makes it extremely difficult to consume enough to meet your daily nutrient requirements and puts your digestive system under a lot of stress. This could harm your health if sustained over a long period.

Another diet is Alternate Day Fasting. This is, as its name suggests, fasting every other day. Again, this seems rather extreme and would not be something I would recommend. Following this protocol would mean going to bed feeling hungry several nights a week, which doesn't sound appealing or sustainable.

The importance of the right nutrition

It may surprise you to learn that your diet accounts for 80% of the body you have. Exercise accounts for 20%.

Being able to enjoy all food groups enables you to be more creative with your meal planning and eat more substantial meals, which will leave you feeling satisfied. And as we have seen, if you are enjoying the process, it's easier to sustain. In addition, when you enjoy the food you eat, your cravings for those 'quick pick-me-up calories' will subside. This, in turn, will help you achieve the body composition you desire.

The great thing about intermittent fasting is it liberates us from obsessing over food. You no longer have to worry about what you can and can't eat or feel deprived of food groups you love but aren't allowed.

Also, if you can enjoy your food in this way when the time comes to fast, you are more likely to do this willingly and with ease.

Although you are intermittent fasting, and there are no forbidden food groups when you are eating, it is crucial to remember that calories do count. Therefore, you cannot achieve your goals by consuming excessive calories in your eating windows.

A balance of all food groups
When creating your meals, balance all food groups. Most of your calories should come from meat, fish, eggs, beans, legumes, and carbohydrates like vegetables, potatoes, steel-cut or rolled oats, and fruit. Try to eat as many whole foods as possible – food that has been processed or refined as little as possible.

Macronutrients
The main food groups are known as micronutrients. Protein, carbohydrates, and fats are our main food groups. Therefore, we want to structure our meals around these three nutrients.

Protein
Protein is essential to our bodies for growth and cell regeneration, producing hormones, and help keep our immune system working effectively.

Protein consists of smaller units known as amino acids. Many of these, known as 'essential amino acids' cannot be created by the body, so they need to be consumed. Some foods are a better source of protein as they provide a better amino acid profile. Animal products are considered a 'complete protein' as they contain all the essential amino acids in the right amounts our bodies need. These foods include meat, poultry, fish, eggs, and dairy products.

Vegetable proteins on their own don't provide adequate amounts of every essential amino acid, but when combined with plant protein sources, they can offer a complete protein profile. Beans, legumes, grains, nuts, and seeds are examples of high-protein plant foods.

Soy and foods derived from soy are rich in protein and contain fibre, vitamins, minerals, and antioxidants, beneficial to our health.

However, there are some concerns about soy and soy products. These include whether they affect a person's thyroid function, disrupt natural hormone levels, particularly estrogen, and cause digestive problems. Although only a few of these concerns are supported by scientific studies, more research is underway.

The importance of protein
A 2006 study published in the American Journal of Clinical Nutrition looked at the effects of macronutrients on the body. They found the most satiating macronutrient was protein. The researchers also found that protein had a positive impact on insulin.
In addition, as protein is slower to digest, it prolongs the feeling of fullness, promoting healthy leptin levels. It also has a higher thermic effect than the other macronutrients, which consume more energy to digest.

Good protein sources
When looking for protein options, look for healthy sources such as:

Lean cuts of meat and poultry: beef, lamb, pork, chicken, turkey.
Fish and shellfish: tuna, salmon, shrimp, rockfish, cod.
Canned fish: such as sardines, mackerel, tuna and salmon.
Cottage cheese and Greek yoghurt (avoid Greek 'style' yoghurts, as these have lower protein and higher sugar levels than the real thing).
Eggs.

Proteins to eat in moderation
Limit the amount of highly processed protein sources you eat. Some examples of highly processed protein include:
Hot dogs, sausages, bacon, corned beef, salami and other processed meats.

Carbohydrates
Carbohydrates are probably the most misunderstood macro-nutrient.

The body breaks down carbohydrates into glucose and releases this into the bloodstream. Glucose levels (also called blood sugar levels) are used as an energy source by cells throughout your body. Unused glucose, stored as glycogen in the liver and muscles, can quickly be converted to glucose for energy.

Carbohydrates are grouped into 'simple' and 'complex'. These terms refer to how quickly the body converts them to glucose. The glycemic index (GI) is a numeric system that ranks how quickly carbohydrates are converted to glucose by the body.

A simple carb converts very quickly and creates sharp spikes in our blood sugar levels. Therefore, simple carbs rank high on the glycemic index. Examples include sugar, soda, white bread, cakes, and many varieties of breakfast cereal. Research has linked regular consumption of high GI foods to an increased risk of heart disease, obesity, and diabetes.

A complex carb converts slowly and ranks low on the glycemic index, and therefore, is considered a "good" carb, as it takes longer to digest and doesn't spike blood sugar levels. Examples include whole porridge oats, whole grains, legumes, vegetables, basmati, and brown rice.

The importance of carbohydrates
In a healthy, balanced diet, carbohydrates should be your body's primary energy source to fuel all its activities, from being active to simply breathing.

You may have heard of people losing a considerable amount of weight when they first embark on a carbohydrate-restricted diet. There is a reason for that.

When the body runs out of carbohydrate reserves, it turns to its glycogen reserves stored in the liver and muscles for energy. Each gram of glycogen is attached to 3 - 4 grams of water. As your body burns through the glycogen stores, the water attached to it is expelled. There's no fat loss. It is just water loss.

This also explains why we can gain back an alarming amount of weight after an indulgent meal. The muscles and liver clawback glycogen with 3 – 4 grams of water per gram of glycogen. In this case, it's not fat gain; it's water gain.

Without carbs, the body is deprived of its primary source of energy. So it turns to its backup source – fat. But that's good, right? Yes. And no.

The problem is, when the body realises you are low on carbs, it starts thinking food is getting scarce. As we discussed earlier, this is when the hormonal imbalances begin to happen. Leptin (fullness hormone) levels fall, ghrelin (hunger hormone) levels rise, and cortisol (stress hormone) levels rise. As a result, your metabolism slows down, and suddenly it becomes difficult to lose weight.

When this happens, even healthy foods can get stored as fat.

Good carbohydrate sources
Whole grain pasta, bread, brown rice.
Oats – rolled oats or steel cut oats are best.
Vegetables – some of the best vegetables are spinach, cauliflower, broccoli, asparagus, greens, brussel sprouts, bell peppers, cabbage, celery, kale, green beans, mushrooms, onions, beetroot and tomatoes.
Fruits – Fresh fruit which is in season is perfect, but do look at your portions, as fruit contains natural sugars (fructose), which in large quantities won't help your weight loss goal. Fruits to enjoy with lower levels of sugar include blueberries, blackberries, strawberries, raspberries and watermelon.
Higher sugar fruits include bananas, mangoes and grapes, and are good before a workout session to provide the body with more energy, or post an exercise session to help the body recover quickly.

Carbohydrates to eat in moderation
As these carbohydrates convert very quickly to sugar in your bloodstream, and provide minimal nutritional value, limiting your consumption of the below foods would be better for your overall health.

White pasta, white bread, bagels.
Pizza, chips, cakes and cookies.
Breakfast cereals and instant oatmeal.
Fruit juices - eat the whole fruit instead, which will provide you with more fibre too.
Dried fruit, jams and preserves.

Fats

A small amount of fat is an essential part of a healthy, balanced diet. Fats are the densest energy source. While protein and carbohydrates contain 4 calories per gram, a gram of fat contains 9 calories. Your body uses fat to absorb other nutrients you feed it, to help maintain cell structure and balance hormone levels.

Fats can be split into three broad categories: saturated fat, unsaturated fat, and trans fat.

Saturated fat sources include meat, salmon, eggs, and dairy products. Aim to keep the amount of saturated fat consumed below 10% of your daily calories.

Unsaturated fat sources include olive oil, avocados, nuts, and sesame oil. If a fat is liquid at room temperature, it is unsaturated fat.

Although nuts are a great source of fat, consume these in moderation. Nuts are very calorie-dense, and overconsumption is very easy and will not help if you want to lose weight.

Trans fat is the fat we want to avoid. This is added to foods to give them a longer shelf life. Packaged pastries, cakes, and fried foods are typically high in trans fats.

The importance of fats

Fats provide our body with a source of essential fatty acids. Essential fatty acids are those the body cannot produce itself, so it relies on getting these from the foods we consume.

Vitamin A, vitamin D, and vitamin E are fat-soluble and rely on these essential fatty acids to be absorbed by our body.

Good fat sources

Even when we are trying to lose weight, our body needs healthy fats to be able to operate effectively and burn our unwanted fat stores. Good sources of fat include:
Avocados and olives.
Oils, such as olive, sesame and ground flaxseed oil.

Fats to eat in moderation

Nuts and peanut butter are good sources of protein and fats; however, they are highly calorific, and can easily be over consumed, so keep an eye on portion sizes.
Butter – look for butter from grass fed cows.

Micro-nutrients

Micro-nutrients are the food groups required in smaller amounts by the body, and all play a vital role in our health and wellbeing.

They are split into three main groups: vitamins, minerals, and antioxidants.

The best way to ensure you are getting as many micronutrients as possible is to consume a colourful range of vegetables, green leafy vegetables, fruits, nuts, and seeds. And add whole grains, beans, legumes, grass-fed, pasture-raised animal products, and wild seafood to your diet.

Below are a few of the essential micro-nutrients.

Iron
Iron is essential for the production of haemoglobin, which helps your blood with oxygen delivery. It also helps strengthen your immune system. Sources include red meat, fish, poultry, oysters, mussels, spinach, and Swiss chard.

Consuming Vitamin C at the same time helps boost your body's ability to absorb more iron.

Magnesium
Magnesium performs several tasks in your body, including regulating your heartbeat, blood pressure and boosting your sleep quality; this mineral is essential for your overall wellbeing.

Research [8] has also shown magnesium has an essential role in insulin action, concluding there is a correlation between low magnesium and insulin resistance. It may also help improve sleep and reduce sugar cravings.

Sources include nuts, seeds, legumes, spinach, and dark chocolate (70-85% cocoa).
A relaxing alternative to boost magnesium levels in the body is to have an Epsom Salt bath.

Sodium
Sodium is an essential mineral needed to maintain fluid balance, nerve impulse contraction, and muscle contraction.

The most common form of sodium is table salt. An adult should consume no more than 6g of salt per day. However, overconsumption is surprisingly easy, as most of the salt we consume is from processed food rather than the salt we add ourselves. Excessive levels of sodium can lead to high blood pressure and heart disease.

Prepare your meals yourself whenever you can, and keep an eye on food labels at other times, so you are aware of your sodium consumption.

Vitamin A
Vitamin A helps protect your vision and keeps your bones and skin healthy alongside other vitamins and minerals.

Sources include eggs, beef, chicken, milk, cheese, and butter. You can also find it in carrots, mangos, pumpkins, as well as dark green vegetables.

How to increase your human growth hormone (HGH) naturally
Consuming foods rich in vitamin C will help boost human growth hormone levels, responsible for healthy muscles, bones, and tissue repair. HGH also has anti-aging qualities.

Foods that are rich in vitamin C sources are oranges, grapefruit, red pepper, kiwi fruit, broccoli, cauliflower, and strawberries.

Foods to support ghrelin
Ghrelin, you may recall, is the 'hunger' hormone, and when we've been restricting calories or carbohydrates, levels of ghrelin increase. Therefore, it is essential to

include many nutrient-dense, unprocessed foods in your diet to help control ghrelin.

Studies have also shown the consumption of fibre also helps to reduce ghrelin production. Kale, spinach, Brussel sprouts, apples, pears, and almonds are good fibre sources.

How to lower insulin resistance naturally
See Magnesium in the Micronutrients section above.

How much should I eat?
To create a healthy body, we need structure, and we need a plan. First, we need to ensure we are eating the right amounts of macronutrients. Secondly, knowing when we will eat allows our body to adapt to our routine and maintain a healthy balance of hormones.

To create the plan, we need to know how many calories we need to eat and split those calories between proteins, carbs, and fats.

Calculating your daily requirements
Many apps and online resources can guide you on your calorie intake and macronutrient split. However, I have found the most effective split for weight loss to be the following. Base this split on your current weight:

Protein - 1.2 grams per one pound of body weight
Carbs - 1 gram per one pound of body weight
Fat – 0.2 grams per one pound of body weight

For example, for a 150 lb woman, her daily plan would look like this:
Protein – 150 x 1.2g = 180 grams of protein per day
Carbs – 150 x 1g = 150 grams of carbs per day

Fat – 150 x 0.2g = 30 grams of fat per day

In terms of calories this equates to 1,590 calories per day.

[Protein 180g x 4 calories = 720. Carbs 150g x 4 calories = 600. Fat 30 g x 9 calories = 270.
Total calories: 720 + 600 + 270 = 1590]

When calculated per the above method, you may find that your daily requirements are more calories than you are currently eating. This may cause you concern and perhaps make you think, "If I'm eating more, won't I gain more weight?".

In the first part of this book, we looked at the impact dieting has on our bodies and how, when we are under-eating, our body compensates by slowing down our metabolism.

The aim is to reset our metabolism to where it should be and realign our hormones. The specific macronutrient breakdown is designed to help you lose weight while firing up that metabolism and resetting hormone levels.

If you have been restricting your calories for a long time, your body will need time to adjust and realise this new eating pattern is consistent and not just another fluctuation on a yo-yo diet.

It may take up to 4 weeks before you start to see some noticeable changes. Don't let that time dishearten you. We are undoing a lot of misalignments, and we are fixing them for good. Keep your eyes on the prize!

You may feel that this is a lot of protein, but a growing number of nutritionists believe the current dietary guidelines for protein are way too low.

A study by John Hopkins University found that a higher protein diet reduced blood pressure and LDL, aka bad cholesterol. While other research found that high protein diets helped prevent obesity, diabetes, and osteoporosis.

As we lose weight, protein is essential in ensuring we lose fat and not muscle.

Split your protein intake evenly across your meals. Research shows that consuming a minimum of 25 grams of protein per meal promotes weight loss, muscle maintenance, and overall health.

In 1997, Yves Boirie conducted a study [9] on fast and slow-digesting proteins. His study concluded that the body fully digested 30g of whey protein in 3-4 hours, and 30g of casein protein took over 7 hours. Somehow, this triggered a popular myth that we need to eat 30 grams of protein every 3 hours; otherwise, we will be breaking down muscle tissue for energy.

However, a study [10] was conducted where two groups were given either 54 grams of protein in one meal or the same amount in 4 smaller meals and monitored over 14 days. It proved the human body is intelligent and adaptable and will take as long as it needs to fully digest and absorb the nutrients it needs from a meal.

If you are struggling to eat the required amount of protein as whole foods, try protein shakes. These are easily portable and can be made on the go, as and when needed. See below for more on protein powder.

Protein powder
Protein powder is a great way to supplement your protein intake; however, not all protein powders are created equally. A good protein powder should provide

you with around 25 grams of protein and a low level of carbs - about 3-4 grams per serving. Watch out for those with higher levels of carbs, as this is mainly sugar.

Many different flavoured options are available, and sources include whey, casein, hemp, mixed plant, soy, pea, and egg protein powders.

Casein is a slow digesting protein. It is a complete protein source, which means it provides all the essential amino acids your body needs for growth and repair. This is an excellent option for the evening. See more in Making your macronutrients work for you later in this chapter.

Whey is a faster-digesting protein, making it ideal to consume an hour or two before a workout.

Like many people, I find whey protein harder to digest. However, I find plant-based protein powder works well. Find what works best for you. Reading reviews of products is also a helpful indicator.

Get a protein shake bottle with a separate screw-on compartment. Put a scoop of your protein powder in the separate compartment and water in the central cup. When you need it, add the powder to the water, give it a shake, and you are good to go.

After consuming a protein shake, avoid drinking lots of water straight after. The protein will take a little while to digest, so the water may make you feel bloated.

Limit your intake of protein powder to a maximum of two servings a day. The rest of your protein intake should come from real food.

Make your macronutrients work for you
Timing of eating carbs
While there is no scientific research that says eating carbs late in the evening will lead to fat gain, there are benefits to limiting your carbs in a late evening meal.

The first reason is when we eat carbs, our body releases insulin to turn these carbs into glucose. We saw that when insulin is released in the body, the human growth hormone (HGH) is inhibited. HGH plays a vital role in cell regeneration, ensuring the healthy growth of muscles, bones, and tissue repair. In addition, the body naturally produces this hormone while we sleep, so if our insulin levels are high at this time, we will limit our levels of HGH.

Secondly, while we are asleep, our body is continually expending energy to keep our body operating. It will use glucose as its first energy source before turning to our fat stores. Elevating our glucose levels before we sleep will reduce how much the body needs to burn fat.

Your last meal of the day
Research shows that it is beneficial to have some slow-digesting protein as your last meal or snack. While you are asleep, your body is busy recovering and regenerating cells; since you are in a fasting state during this period, it ensures your body has enough amino acids to perform its functions.

Protein powders are a great option here. For example, try whisking chocolate protein powder with almond milk and water (using less liquid than you would for a shake) to make a great-tasting mousse dessert.

See above for more information on protein powders.

Creating your meal plan
Creating your daily plan for weight loss

It's essential to create a plan for your daily intake of food. It is so easy to eat an extra 100 – 200 calories a day, which will take you off track if you are not planning your meals.

Now, it might feel a bit complicated at first, but believe me, after you have got this down once, it will be easy, and you will soon fall into a natural routine of knowing when and what you are eating.

I find it best to use a spreadsheet for this initially. Along the top, label the columns with days of the week. Along the side, mark the columns with times of day you will be eating. You may choose to eat 3, 4, or perhaps 5 times a day. Try to keep these meal times consistent, so your body can develop a rhythm.

Start by splitting your protein grams between each planned meal. It doesn't have to be an exact even split, as you'll see in the example below.

Create a few meals you will enjoy around a protein source, adding in suitable carbs and fats to complement the protein. Then slot these meals into your spreadsheet, adding the protein, carbs, and fat grams of each meal. The total protein, carbs, and fat for each day will equal the daily requirements you calculated earlier. Play around with this until you get a balance of meals you like that total up to your daily needs.

Begin by creating a few meal ideas that you can easily interchange as lunch or dinner options. Have a few meals to keep your diet varied but simple enough to keep your shopping list easy to manage at the start.

Doing this will also help you get settled into your new plan quickly. Refer to the 'simple meal ideas' in the Tips, Tricks, and Tools section of the book for some inspiration.

As you get into a routine and accustomed to your daily food intake, it will be easier to get creative and add new meal options.

There are many apps available to help with the nutritional breakdown of foods. For example, MyFitnessPal has a huge food database, a recipe importer, and a barcode scanner. Fooducate is another app that measures the calorie quality of food, and if an item has a low food grade, it will offer you healthier alternatives. And you can, of course, use a search engine to find out the nutritional value of foods by portion size.

Using the example from above, our 150 lb woman will be eating 180 grams of protein. Say she wants to spread this over 5 'meals', that's 30 grams of protein per meal.

Following the 14:10 eating protocol: eating within a 10-hour window, her day could look like this:

	MON				**TUES**
		Protein	**Carbs**	**Fat**	
11 am	protein oats with chia seeds and apple	35	55	10	
2 pm	chicken breast salad with sweet potato	40	60	-	
4 pm	plain Greek yoghurt with a tiny drizzle of honey and mixed berries	20	15	5	
7 pm	sesame seed tuna steak with stir fried veggies	50	15	12	
9 pm	protein mousse (see above)	35	5	3	
	Daily total macro nutrients	**180**	**150**	**30**	

If you follow the 5:2 or Eat Stop Eat diets, use the above to guide your standard eating day plan. As you are not restricted to eating within a 10-hour window, you can adjust the timings to suit your needs.

Starting out

1. Give your body time to adjust

One of the clever aspects of ghrelin is it becomes connected to your usual meal times. For example, if you usually eat breakfast at 8 am, lunch at 1 pm, and dinner at 7 pm, your body will release the ghrelin hormone at those times, making you feel hungry.

When you change your meal times, it may take a few days for your body to get used to your new routine. Just allow your body time to adjust.

Similarly, if you are used to eating only 2 meals and decide to start eating 4 smaller meals, you may find you won't be hungry at the appropriate times. Do eat at these times, though. But, again, give your body time to adjust, and it will soon start releasing ghrelin at these new intervals.

Results aren't going to happen overnight; give your body time to catch up with your new routine and rebalance your hormones in response.

2. Give yourself time to adjust
Be kind to yourself. If this is new to you, give yourself time to adjust.

If you slip up a few times, that's ok, don't put too much pressure on yourself to get this 'exactly right'. You have taken the most significant step, which is starting.

Changing our habits is more challenging because it is more of a conscious effort to do these new things. However, with practice and repetition, the actions become more natural; they sink into our subconscious and become effortless over time.

We've had to learn how to do most of the things that now come naturally to us. For example, think about walking, speaking, and learning to drive. How easy and naturally do these things come to you now? Sometimes we can drive from A to B and don't even recall the journey!

It will just take a little time and practice to become a habit and feel more natural. Refer to the 'You – Getting across the finish line' chapter for more guidance.

> *Motivation gets you going; habit gets you there – Zig Ziglar*

3. Stay hydrated

60% of our body is made up of water, making it essential to stay hydrated to maintain good health and proper body function. In addition, our brain is approximately 85% water and is very sensitive to the amount of water available. You may have noticed this when you have been dehydrated and suffered a headache.

Staying hydrated is particularly important when fasting. Around 20-30% of our water intake comes from food, so we need to compensate for that by drinking additional fluids.

Water, green and herbal tea, and black coffee are permitted while fasting.

It is recommended we drink eight 8-ounce glasses of water which equates to about 2 litres. Try adding a slice of lemon, lime, or cucumber to your water to add a little flavour. Get into the habit of drinking a full glass of water within 30 minutes of waking up.

Try not to exceed 3 cups of coffee a day, and avoid caffeine in the evenings, as this may interfere with getting a good night's sleep.

As well as keeping you hydrated, a glass of water, tea, or coffee can also help stave off hunger for a little longer. And, now I've mentioned it: hunger pangs – don't worry, they do not build up, and build up, into a giant unbearable crescendo! Instead, they will come and go.

4. Watch out for 'hidden' calories

It is easy to overlook those small dressings and additions, but those additional calories soon add up:

Olive oil – 2 tablespoons = 238 calories
Mayonnaise – 2 tablespoons = 188 calories
Cream – 2 tablespoons = 137 calories
Butter – 1 tablespoon = 102 calories

It's so easy to miss these calories off your count, and yet these hidden calories can be detrimental to your weight loss goals. The best way to be aware of these calories is to prepare your meals yourself. And when eating out, ask for all dressings to be served on the side.

5. Minimise overly processed, refined food

For most of us, cutting out processed foods from our diets forever would be unrealistic. So, minimise the consumption of these foods.

Highly processed foods usually taste delicious, but they are frequently high in calories and low in nutritional value. In addition, studies show that our leptin hormone, the one that signals we are full, doesn't work well when we eat highly processed food; therefore, these empty calories can also trigger overeating.

Examples of overly processed foods include cakes, cookies, pastries, doughnuts, soda, and sweetened beverages, pizza, white bread, chocolate, candy, and ice cream.

If you can, cut these out for the first 21 days of implementing your new plan - this will help your body become adjusted to your new way of eating.

After that, aim to limit these foods to once or twice a week. After the three-week break from them, you will find you appreciate the 'indulgence' more, and, quite possibly, you may even surprise yourself that they no longer taste as good as you once thought.

6. Make life easier on yourself

If stir-frying vegetables, add your fish or chicken or other protein sources to the same pan. If you are roasting chicken, eat it with roasted vegetables and perhaps a little sweet potato. If you are steaming fish, steam your vegetables and a couple of new potatoes in at the same time. If it's something you could enjoy cold, cook a double portion, and have it for lunch the next day.

7. Alcohol

Yes, you can still drink alcohol: it is unnecessary to cut alcohol out completely, nor would it be much fun.

Alcohol is primarily empty calories, meaning for the calories, they provide little nutritional value. Pure alcohol contains 7 calories per gram – almost as much as a gram of fat, at 9 calories per gram. On top of this, your body cannot store alcohol in the way it can store protein and carbs, so your body needs to prioritise burning the calories consumed through alcohol first. While it's doing this, your fat burning is put on hold.

So, the bottom line is to find the right balance to enjoy the odd glass and achieve the body you want.

8. Dealing with challenges

You are going to face some challenges or temptations. Life happens. Perhaps these have derailed you in the past? The best way to push through these is to visualise how you will respond to them in advance. This way, when put on the spot, you already have your rehearsed solution on hand and can continue moving in the right direction.

And what happens if you fall off the wagon? Whatever you do, don't beat yourself up. Instead, think of what triggered you to fall off the wagon and different actions you could take the next time it happens. And then simply start again.

9. Enjoy the process
You have just waved goodbye to restrictive dieting. You no longer have to banish your favourite foods forever from your life. You've said goodbye to your metabolism operating at a snail's pace. And you are no longer throwing your hormones off balance. Instead, food can now become enjoyable and pleasurable, as it was always meant to be.

If you are struggling to get started
If you are struggling to get started with intermittent fasting, here are some tips to help you ease into it gradually. But, of course, these are only to be used as a last resort!

1. **If you opt for the 14:10 (16:8 for men) diet**
   Start with fasting for just 12 hours, giving you an eating window of 12 hours. Then, after a week or two, change this to a 13-hour fast, 11-hour eating window. Then you can fully transition to the 14:10 a week or two after that.

2. **If you are opting for the 5:2 diet**
   Start your fast days with a higher calorie allowance. For example:

Week 1 & 2: begin with a 1,000-calorie allowance on your two fast days
Week 3 & 4: drop to an 800-calorie allowance on your two fast days
Week 5 & 6 lower to a 650-calorie allowance on your two fast days.

Depending on your previous calorie intake, you may already be seeing significant changes in your body. This should help you transition fully to the 500-calorie allowance on the two fast days.

If you find you are happy with the rate of weight loss at any of the above stages, stick to that stage.

3. **If you have opted for the Eat Stop Eat diet**
   Snacking on raw vegetable crudites and low sugar fruit such as berries during your fasting period may help.

4. **If you still can't get started**
   As a very last option, you could try random meal skipping. This option is a highly customizable type of intermittent fasting but with fewer constraints. As its name suggests, you pick random meals and skip them.64

   Meal skipping could be an option if you don't have a regular schedule or think the other versions of intermittent fasting would work for you.

   It may also be a suitable alternative for people who aren't quite ready to commit to one of the above fasting options yet, offering a way to test it out and ease into it.

   It's important to realize that as you may not be fasting for an extended period, it's unlikely you will reap the full benefits of the other intermittent fasting methods.

Stepping it up a notch

Carb cycling

When you are ready, consider introducing carb cycling to your routine. This section will be particularly beneficial when you pair it with the "Stepping it up a notch" in the Exercise section.

We have heard the short-term benefits of restricting carbs: our body turns to its fat stores for energy. However, we also know that when carbs are restricted over a continuous period, their impact on our metabolism and hormonal balance is detrimental to our health and well-being.

Carb cycling is a way of reaping the benefits without misaligning our hormones or slowing down our metabolism.

How carb cycling works

We can use carb cycling to have higher levels of carbs on one day, followed by lower levels of carbs the following day. We can repeat this cycle as often as we choose.

Research shows that the most efficient way to accelerate the body's ability to burn fat is to lower carb intake while increasing fat intake.

On all days, protein consumption should remain the same.
However, you will make adjustments between carbs and fat. When you are on a low-carb day, increase your fats. When you are on a high-carb day, decrease your fats. As a gram of fat has over double the calories of a gram of carbs, you can trade one gram of fat for two grams of carbs. We will look at an example below.

Carb cycling is a great way to accelerate fat loss while at the same time being able to eat your favourite foods. By cycling through on low and high carb days, you burn fat without your metabolism slowing down, causing you to hit a plateau, which means you can get rid of that stubborn belly fat and fat around your flanks and hips without the fear of gaining it back later.

How to implement carb cycling
Adjust your diet to include more carbs on days that you are training with weights, body weight, or resistance training: on these days, fat consumption is lowered.

What happens in your body? Leptin (fullness hormone) levels rise, ghrelin (hunger hormone) levels lower, and your metabolism is cranked up.

Now instead of allowing our bodies to become used to this higher carb intake and start storing these extra carbs – we surprise it. The next day we limit our carb intake.

A good day to have a lower carb intake is when you are HIIT training, resting, or fasting. Adjust your diet on these days to include fewer carbs and more fat. Your metabolism will be supercharged from the previous high-carb day, so once your body has burned the lower level of carbs you have eaten, it will switch to burn your stored fat for energy.

Before your body thinks it needs to slow down your metabolism to be in line with a reduced level of carbs, you surprise it again, and you switch to a higher carb day.

In the example we had above, for a 150 lb woman, the daily plan looked like this:

Protein – 150 x 1.2g = 180 grams of protein per day
Carbs – 150 x 1g = 150 grams of carbs per day
Fat – 150 x 0.2g = 30 grams of fat per day

This equates to 1,590 calories per day.

To create a low carb day, keep protein levels the same, and replace most carbs with healthy sources of fat, for example, avocados, eggs, and smoked salmon. Carbs should come mainly from vegetables and lower-sugar fruits like berries.

Rest days and HIIT training days are good days to go low carb.

A **low carb/high fat** day would look like this:
Protein – 180 grams of protein
Carbs – 50 grams of carbs
Fat – 70 grams of fat

This equates to 1,550 calories per day.
[Calculated (180 x 4) + (50 x 4) + (70 x 9) = 1,550 calories]

A **high carb/low fat** day would look like this:
Protein – 180 grams of protein
Carbs – 170 grams of carbs
Fat – 20 grams of fat

This equates to 1,550 calories per day.
[Calculated (180 x 4) + (170 x 4) + (20 x 9) = 1,580 calories]

When you have reached your target weight

Creating your daily plan for maintenance
Once you have reached your target weight, you will want to adjust your macronutrient consumption to maintain your weight at that level.

Based on your new weight, adjust as follows:
Protein - 1 gram per one pound of body weight
Carbs - 1.5 grams per one pound of body weight
Fat – 0.25 gram per one pound of body weight

For a 130 lb woman, the daily **maintenance** plan would look like this:
Protein – 130 grams of protein per day
Carbs – 195 grams of carbs per day
Fat – 32 grams of fat per day
In terms of calories, this equates to 1,600 calories per day.

How to break a plateau

Sometimes the number on the scale hasn't budged, but before you start to feel disheartened, take a look in the mirror. How do your clothes fit – are they getting looser? Your waist, hip, and thigh measurements – are they going down?

If the answer is yes, then you are doing everything right. What you are doing is replacing fat with muscle. Muscle weighs more than fat. So, although the scales may not be changing – you are. Body composition is more important than body weight.

If the answer is no, here are some factors that may need reviewing:

Track your food intake
You may be consuming more calories than you think. For a few days, measure and track everything you eat to pinpoint if this is the case.

Remember to include liquid calories in your calorie count, as these are frequently missed. Swap fruit juice for the whole fruit instead.

Carb cycling
If you haven't already, try carb cycling. Refer to the 'How to implement carb cycling' in the Nutrition section.

Reduce stress levels
As we saw earlier, levels of cortisol (the stress hormone) and ghrelin (the hunger hormone) increase in direct response to stressful situations, which explains why many people tend to overeat when stressed. When this cycle perpetuates over time, it can increase appetite, particularly for 'comfort food', and may lead to higher consumption of alcohol, less sleep, and being less active.

To move away from this cycle, we first need to identify the root cause - is there anything we can do to eliminate these stresses? Then, we also need to find ways to manage stressful times. Some activities that may help are:

1. **Bath** – take time out to enjoy a relaxing bath. Adding Epsom Salts to the water gives you the additional benefit of boosting your magnesium levels.
2. **Sauna or steam room** – the heat causes the muscles to relax, improves blood circulation, and detoxifies.

3. **Belly breathing** – sit or lie down comfortably. Place one hand on your belly and one on your heart. Take a long, slow breath allowing your belly to expand. Hold for a second, and then exhale gently. Repeat a few times. This simple exercise can help relieve tension, slows the heartbeat, and helps calm a racing mind.
4. **Meditation** – meditation calms the mind and body. There are many different ways to meditate, including mindfulness, breathing, spiritual, and movement, such as yoga. You can practice meditation on your own, in a group, or with guidance. There are many resources available online to help you choose which type of meditation may suit you.
5. **Take time out** – enjoy some quality time with friends and family. Laughter is a great stress reliever.
6. **Go for a walk** – a walk through a park - without headphones, so you can enjoy nature at its best – can help you get out of your head!

Getting a good night's sleep

Getting enough good quality sleep each night isn't just nice to have; it's a must-have for your health and wellbeing. Aim to get 7-8 hours each night.

Lack of sleep lowers your leptin levels (your 'full up' hormone) and increases your ghrelin levels (your 'hunger' hormone) -the exact opposite of what we want to achieve to lose weight.

To create better sleeping habits, go to bed and wake up at the same time every day – including weekends, and avoid eating or drinking late in the evenings, especially coffee and alcohol. Being active during the day can also help you sleep better at night.

Have your thyroid checked
If you cannot attribute it to anything else, it may be worth consulting with your doctor to check your thyroid and see if it is underactive, also known as hypothyroidism.
An underactive thyroid means your thyroid gland isn't producing enough thyroid hormones. Too little thyroid hormone slows down your body's metabolism, and you will find it difficult to lose weight. Common symptoms include tiredness and weight gain.

Hypothyroidism is a more common issue amongst women than men and increases over the age of 50. Family history may also contribute as a factor.
Up to 60 million Americans struggle with weight loss due to a thyroid issue. And according to the British Thyroid Foundation, it affects one in twenty people.
Your GP can treat hypothyroidism with a hormone replacement tablet.

How to increase your protein intake

While this isn't a cookbook, I wanted to give you some simple meal ideas. These ideas may be of use to those whose protein intake has suddenly increased, and you are wondering how to meet those needs! The key is to build your plan around the foods you enjoy.

Where possible, prepare double portions, one for dinner and one for the next day's lunch, saving time and additional meal planning.

Eggs

Eggs are so versatile, and you can enjoy scrambled, boiled, or poached.

Get creative with omelettes. Try adding different combinations of chopped bell peppers, courgettes, mushrooms, spinach, leeks, tomatoes, shrimp, lobster, salmon, ricotta, or cheddar cheese. The list is endless, and omelettes are such a quick and easy way of creating a meal.

The protein is in the egg white in eggs, and the fat, vitamins and other nutrients are in the yolk. So, to keep the protein levels high and the fat level lower, make an omelette with 3 or 4 eggs, but discard 1 or 2 of the egg yolks

Fish & seafood

With such a wide variety of fish and seafood available, it is easy to create varied meals simply by cooking differently: grill, roast, steam, or even pan-fry in a little coconut oil or sesame oil. Add lemon or lime juice for additional flavour, and pumpkin or other seeds for an extra crunch.

Try coating a tuna steak with sesame seeds, and pan-fry with a little oil. Serve with stir-fried vegetables and bean shoots.

Alternatively, wrap a salmon fillet in foil, place it in a steamer. After 4 minutes, add broccoli and cauliflower florets - steam for a further 6 minutes. Finally, grate cucumber, chop some mint leaves and add to full-fat Greek yoghurt for a refreshing dressing for the salmon.

Grilled skewers

Thread chicken, fish, seafood, or tofu alternately with veggies onto skewers and grill. Remember to soak wooden skewers in cold water beforehand to prevent them from burning.

Try mixing chunky peanut butter, low sodium soy sauce, crushed garlic, and lime juice for a quick and easy chicken satay sauce.

One-pot casserole

After the prep, one-pot casseroles are great, as they take care of themselves. So, while they may take a while longer to cook, the preparation is quick and easy.

For example, heat a little oil in a casserole dish. Add stewing lamb, carrots, celery, leeks, and potatoes, all chopped into similar-sized chunks. Cook on the hob for 5 mins, browning the lamb. Add lamb or vegetable stock, cover, and cook in the oven for 90 mins at 150° Celsius.

Protein oats

Take half a cup of rolled or steel-cut oats, and top with boiling water, just enough to cover the oats. Leave to cool. Make up a protein shake with coconut or almond milk, and add one tablespoon of milled chia seeds. Mix the oats into the protein shake. Refrigerate. Top with a few blueberries to serve, creating a great post-workout meal.

Stir-fries

Stir-fries are a quick and easy way of creating a nutritious meal in one pan, using various vegetables, together with your chosen protein, perhaps fish, chicken, beef, tofu, or seafood.

Adding garlic, ginger, a little reduced-sodium soy sauce, or a drizzle of teriyaki or hoisin sauce can create varied and delicious meals in minutes.

Supplements – not necessary, but...

Taking many supplements isn't necessary if you have a well-balanced and healthy diet from a wide range of whole fresh foods. A good diet should provide you with all the nutrients your body needs.

However, you may choose to take some or all of the following if you feel your diet lacks some of the critical sources, and your levels might be low.

Most supplements are absorbed better by your body when taken with food. Check the labels for instructions.

Magnesium
Please refer to the micronutrients section for the function and benefits of magnesium.
Sources include nuts, seeds, legumes, spinach, and dark chocolate (70-85% cocoa).

Multivitamin
There is much debate around whether it is necessary to supplement our diet with multivitamin pills. Expert opinions vary between supporting consumption as part of a healthy lifestyle and focussing on your diet first to ensure you get all the nutrients you need.
This one is a matter of personal choice.

Omega 3
Omega 3 is needed to support the health of our eyes, brain, heart, and joints. Unfortunately, the body

cannot produce Omega 3, so getting this from your diet is vital.

Sources include oily fish such as salmon, mackerel, and sardines. Flax seeds, chia seeds, and walnuts are also good sources.

Vitamin C
Vitamin C has many functions, including supporting our immune system and helping the body absorb iron from our diet. However, the body cannot produce this vitamin itself, so we need to include rich sources into our diet.

Sources include bell peppers, broccoli, cauliflower, spinach, and kiwi fruit.

Vitamin D
Getting enough Vitamin D is essential for strong, healthy bones, as it helps your body absorb calcium, necessary for bone growth. It also strengthens muscles and supports your immune system.

During the spring and summer months, most people can get sufficient levels of Vitamin D through sunlight and eating a balanced diet.

During the autumn and winter months, this may not be so easy to achieve. However, a daily supplement during these months may help you sustain healthy levels of this vitamin.

Sources include wild-caught fish, tinned tuna and sardines, egg yolks, milk, and yoghurt.

EXERCISE
20% of the equation

Why long cardio sessions don't work

For years, the weight-loss advice we have been given has focused on low-to-moderate aerobic activity, such as jogging or running 30–60 minutes every day.

The thinking behind this goes hand in hand with the information on restrictive dieting. That is: to lose weight, you need to eat less and move more. We have seen what eating less does to your body in the previous chapters. So now, let's debunk the myth that long, steady-state cardio sessions are good for you.

For starters, long, drawn-out cardio sessions raise our cortisol levels (the stress hormone). Yale University published a study [3] that showed women with excess belly fat have an exaggerated cortisol response. So, if you are going for a 45-minute run, the increase in cortisol causes you to store even more fat.

Research over the past decade reports that these long sessions increase ghrelin (our hunger hormone) and decrease leptin (our fullness hormone), causing us to want to eat even more. The long and constant pounding on the treadmill can also damage our back, knees, and hips and age us faster. Combine this with a calorie-restrictive diet, and your body won't have enough fuel for muscle and tissue repair, and that's when you can start to suffer from injuries.

Steady-state cardio does not work. These long sessions can do more harm than good when we look at our hormonal balance and long-term health. Exercising this way may have been stalling your progress. However, we still need to exercise.

The lymphatic system is part of our circulatory and immune systems and helps our body eliminate waste. The lymphatic system depends mainly on muscle activity in the body for its circulation. When the lymph flow becomes stagnant, waste builds up, leading to weight gain, bloat, and cellulite. A study by Stanford University reported that a lymphatic slowdown causes fat storage to double, so it is vital for our well-being to keep active and exercise.

Burn fat in 10-minute cardio sessions

Rather than long, drawn-out cardio sessions, opt for short, intense burst training – known as high-intensity interval training (HIIT) - it is one of the best ways to burn belly fat and lose weight and can be done in minutes!

The energy to fuel your workouts comes from the breakdown of glycogen, which is stored in your muscles. With HIIT training, as your heart rate increases, fat is released from the body's stores to help fuel the workout. The release of fat reaches its peak within 10 – 15 minutes.

HIIT training positively affects ghrelin and leptin levels, so it helps our fat loss goals by managing our hunger and eating hormones.

A study by the University of Bath tested various hormone levels in individuals who participated in 30-second sprint intervals. At the end of the intervals, ghrelin had decreased and was significantly lower even after 30 minutes of recovery than they were pre-exercise. It also showed the human growth hormone levels were higher. This hormone can promote weight loss.

Apart from keeping our hormones in balance, HIIT training can also help us burn more fat – even when we are not exercising. This is due to the principles of excess post-exercise oxygen consumption (EPOC), which you may have heard of as the 'afterburn effect".

EPOC

When HIIT training, your body consumes more oxygen than you have, creating an oxygen deficit, which you will encounter as huffing and puffing.

After you exercise, it takes some time for your body to return to your normal resting state or your resting metabolic rate. During this post-workout window, your body works like crazy to get your breathing and heart rate back to normal and replenish your oxygen stores. In addition, it is busy repairing any damaged muscle and connective tissue, clearing waste from your muscles, and refilling them with fuel.

You may also notice that you sweat and keep on sweating, even after you've finished exercising. This is your body's mechanism to keep you cool during the energy-demanding process of recovery. All this accounts for why EPOC burns so much fat.

Studies [11,12,13,14] show that although this process happens after long, steady-state cardio, the afterburn process lasts just a few minutes. So basically, once you are off that treadmill, your body stops burning extra calories.

Compare this to a short, swift burst of HIIT training – typically around 10 minutes – and the afterburn effect can last up to 24 hours post-workout, sometimes even longer. Not bad for a 10-minute effort!

HIIT in the gym – can be performed on the treadmill, exercise bikes, elliptical trainers, and rowing machines.

An alternative to sprinting on the treadmill is to walk at a fast pace and on an incline. Note: if you choose this option, do not hold on to the handrail for support: this defeats the whole object of challenging your body.

HIIT at home – get your heart pumping with burpees, mountain climbers, jumping jacks, plank jacks, jump squats, high knee jogging on the spot.

How often should you aim to do HIIT training sessions? Each week, you can safely do 2-3 HIIT workout sessions of 10 to 20-minute durations. Exercising this way will enable your body to fully recover, as well as allow you to lose a good amount of fat.

HIIT interval timings

These will be different based on your fitness levels.

- Beginners could start at a 1:2 exercise to recovery ratio. For example, exercise hard for 20 seconds, recover for 40 seconds. Repeat this cycle for 10 repetitions.
- As you progress, work towards a 1:1 ratio. For example, this could be 30 seconds of intense exercise; recover for 30 seconds. Repeat this cycle for 10 – 20 repetitions.
- As you improve further, you can gradually increase 45 seconds of intense exercise, and recover for 30 seconds. Repeat this cycle for 10 – 16 repetitions.

You want to work hard enough and long enough to be out of breath during the intense interval.

The recovery interval needs to be long enough to get your breathing back under control – but no longer. Keep your body moving during this recovery period:

- Slow down your sprint to walking on a treadmill.
- Lower the resistance or incline if you are on the rower or elliptical.
- Try on the spot marching for at-home exercises.

Start your sessions with a 5-minute warm-up, and end your sessions with a 5-minute cooldown, and remember to stretch out the muscles you've worked. In total, the intense/recovery sessions can last 10 – 20 minutes. Top and tail this with your warm-up, cool down, and stretch.

There are many free interval timer apps available, where you can adjust the interval settings, set up several routines, and even track your activity over the months. Interval Timer is one such app.

Whatever exercise you are doing, do it safely. Ensure you are consuming enough nutrients and water to fuel your session and stay hydrated: both during and after your workout.

Stagger your workouts, so if you are doing high-intensity training on one day, aim for a lower-intensity activity the next. Give your muscles a chance to recover before you push them again. Recovery will help you avoid injury, fatigue, and muscle soreness.

Fasted workouts
For those considering fasted workouts, I believe the benefits of fuelling your body before a workout far outweigh any benefits of exercising in a fasted state.

If you really must exercise in a fasted state, take 10g of BCAA pre-workout. BCAA (Branched Chain Amino Acids) is a supplement to support protein synthesis by helping the body build new muscle tissue and can decrease muscle damage.

Strength and resistance exercises

Our metabolic rate is at its highest during periods of growth when we are young. Then, as we get older, our metabolic rate slows down at a rate of between 2% - 5% per decade, after the age of 40. The decrease is partly due to a natural decline in muscle mass – and we can do something about that!

Even when we are resting, muscle burns 3 times more calories than fat. So, let's swap that fat for some lean muscle!

Women produce a fraction of the testosterone that men do, so don't worry about creating big, bulky muscles. To do that, we would need to live in the weights room and supplement like crazy.

Working out at home
You don't need to go to the gym for a lean, toned body. Nor do you need expensive exercise equipment. Instead, you can simply use your body weight as resistance or grab a couple of water bottles as weights. Alternatively, you may want to purchase some of the following to help.

Resistance bands
Exercise bands are a great tool to add resistance to your exercises and stretches. They are lightweight and portable, so they are fantastic to pop into your bag when traveling. Get a set with different resistance levels for various muscle groups and increase the resistance as you get stronger.

Adjustable ankle/wrist weights
These are a great option and very versatile. Choose weights with zipped compartments with individual weight bags. The weights can then be removed to work smaller muscle groups, and added as you strengthen your larger muscles.

Hula hoop
A weighted hula hoop is a fun way to tighten and tone your abs and whittle away your waist. Start gently for a couple of minutes to begin with, as you may find you

will get some bruising for the first few days as your body gets used to it. Build up gradually. Take turns spinning your hula hoop clockwise and counter-clockwise to work your body evenly. Also, allow yourself plenty of room – a one-metre circumference hoop will need a two-metre space to rotate.

Yoga mat
A yoga mat will help when doing floor exercises. Choose one with a non-slip surface and one that can be easily rolled up when not in use. A thickness of 5mm provides a perfect balance of protecting your body and a firm enough base to balance and connect with the floor.

Exercises

The strength and resistance exercises below will help you create lean, toned muscle.
It is essential to do these exercises correctly. As it is easier to see this visually rather than narrated, I recommend you watch videos on YouTube for these exercises to familiarise yourself with the correct form.
You can do these exercises with your body weight, resistance bands, or weights.

Shape your butt

Glute bridges
The glutes (butt) stabilise your pelvis and hips. However, if your glutes are not strong enough, they will call on your back muscles to help; this throws your body out of balance and explains why so many people suffer lower back and hip pain.

Glute bridges are one of the best exercises you can do. They not only target your glutes; they also strengthen your core and back. It is very easy to get this exercise wrong, though. To activate your glutes correctly, try using a resistance band around your thighs, just above your knees.

Lay down, arms by your side, knees bent, and feet flat on the floor. You should just about be able to touch your heels with your fingertips. Then, digging your heels into the floor, lift your butt, so your upper body and thighs form a straight line while at the same time actively pushing your knees outwards against the resistance band. Hold for a count of 2, and return gently back to the floor, pushing against the resistance band throughout the exercise. That is one repetition. Work up gradually to 3 sets of 10 repetitions. You should feel the burn in your glutes!

As you progress, a slight variation is to hold at the top of the bridge and push and release your knees against the resistance band 5 times before lowering back to the floor.

OPEN GLUTE BRIDGE

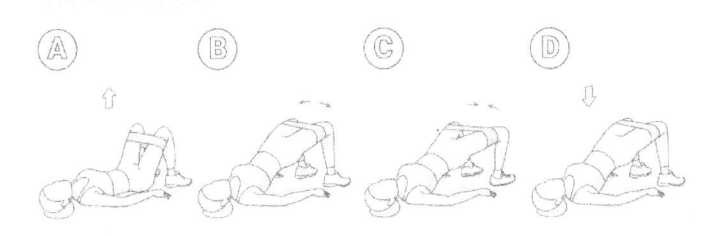

Donkey kicks
Start on your hands and knees, with knees and feet hip-width apart and hands directly beneath your shoulders. Brace your core, and don't let your back arch.

Lift one leg in line with your body, keeping the knee bent at 90 degrees so the sole of your foot is facing the ceiling. From that position, lift the leg as high as possible, lower, then lift back up, repeat 20 times. Switch legs, and repeat. Work towards 2 sets of 20 repetitions per leg.

As you progress, add in ankle weights or resistance bands.

To make this exercise harder, perform the donkey kicks with a straight leg.

A variation of this exercise is great for working the sides of your butt, which is especially good if you suffer with hip dips: instead of lowering your knee to the starting position, lower it diagonally, so it crosses over the back of the opposite leg, then lift and repeat. Aim to complete 2 sets of 20 repetitions per leg.

DONKEY KICK

WITH RESISTANCE BAND

Ⓐ Ⓑ

Fire hydrants

This exercise has the same starting position as the donkey kicks. You lift your leg outwards to the side this time, keeping the bent leg at a 90-degree angle. Lift the leg as high as you can while keeping your hips level. Work towards 20 repetitions per set and 2 sets per leg. You can add resistance bands or ankle weights as you progress.

FIRE HYDRANT

Clamshell

Lay on your right side, with your arm supporting your head. Keep your legs bent at an angle and your feet in line with your butt. Keeping your core engaged, your hips still, and your feet together, raise your left knee, and then lower back down. Work up towards 15 repetitions and 2 sets per leg.

For a more advanced workout, use a resistance band across your thighs.

A twist on this exercise is to complete it with your feet raised off the ground for the whole set duration.

CLAMSHELL EXERCISE
WITH RESISTANCE BAND

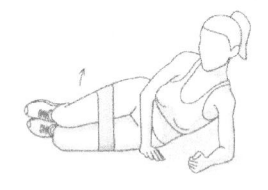

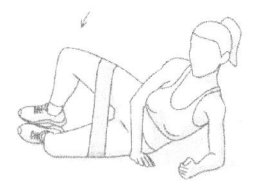

Work those legs

Squats

Standing up, position your feet between hip and shoulder-width apart, with your toes pointing outwards at a slight angle. Relax your shoulders. Clasp your hands in front of you at chest level for balance.
Although your feet are flat on the floor, keep the weight in your heels.

Keeping your feet still, lower your hips down as far as possible, as if you are about to sit on a chair. Make sure your knees stay in alignment with your heels. Hold for 2 seconds, return to starting position, pushing up through your heels. That's one repetition. Work up gradually to 3 sets of 15 repetitions.
Pushing up through your heels engages your leg and glute muscles and protects your knees.

A variation is to position your feet in a slightly wider position and squat from there. The wider stance will target your inner thigh muscles more.

As you progress, hold a weight to your chest with crossed arms. The weight will challenge your leg and core muscles to work harder, and keeping the weight close to your body will protect your back.

SQUATS

Lunges

Lunges are another excellent exercise for your legs, and because they focus on staying balanced, they are also a great core workout.

Stand with your feet together and your hands on your hips for balance. Take a big step forward with your right leg. Your left heel will be off the floor. You are keeping your body upright as you lower down, bending both legs. Make sure your right knee stays in line with your heel. Straighten both legs up, and step your right leg back, so you have both feet together, keeping your stomach muscles engaged throughout the exercise. That is one rep - work towards completing 2 sets of 15 repetitions on each leg.

Suppose you struggle with your balance: after you have straightened both legs back up, lower back down from this position, rather than returning to the starting position after each rep. Rest your fingertips on the back of a chair for extra balance if you need to.

As you progress, hold weights in your hands for an extra challenge.

Lift and firm your bust

Working your chest muscles (pectoralis major and minor) will improve your posture and help lift and support your bust.

Classic and Kneeling Push up

The best exercise is the classic push-up. Lay face down on the floor, place your hands under, but slightly wider than your shoulders. Straighten your arms; your body weight is supported by your toes and your hands, your body in a straight line: this is your starting position.

Bending your arms, lower your body to the floor, keeping your elbows tucked in close to your body and your body straight. Straighten your arms to return to your starting position.

Lower your knees to the floor and keep the upper body movements the same as above to make this easier.

KNEE PUSH-UPS

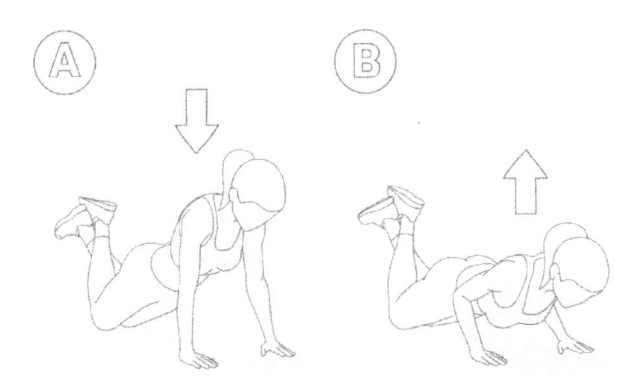

If, like me, the thought of press-ups makes you want to move on to the next section, try these instead:

Bear Plank Shoulder Tap

Start on the floor, on your hands and knees, hands directly under shoulders, and knees directly under hips.

Now, using your toes and hands to support your body weight, hover your knees 2 inches off the floor: this is your starting position.

Keeping your body still in this position, lift your right hand to tap your left shoulder. Return your hand to the floor. Repeat with your left hand to your right shoulder. That's one repetition. Work up to 2 sets of 15 reps.

To progress, take this to a full plank position as illustrated below.

PLANK SHOULDER TAPS

(A) **(B)**

Weighted floor press

For this exercise, you will need arm weights around your wrist, light hand weights, or a couple of bottles of water.

Lie on the floor on your back, knees bent, feet flat on the floor. Bend your arms, and keep your upper arms and elbows on the floor, in line with your shoulders with your chosen weights: this is your starting position. Now lift and straighten both arms to the ceiling, keeping them in line with your shoulders. Return to the starting position. That is one rep. Aim for 2 sets of 20 reps.

Walk tall, back exercises

Weak back muscles cause poor posture. Walk tall with these exercises.

Superman

Lie face down on the floor, with straight legs and your arms outstretched in front of you: this is your starting position.

Raise your arms and legs 10-15cm off the floor at the same time, being careful not to strain your neck. Only raise your arms and legs as high as you can comfortably do so. Hold for 5 seconds, and return to the starting position. That's one rep.

Aim for 2 sets of 5 repetitions.

If this is too difficult, do this exercise with one arm and the opposite leg at a time. Then swap to the other arm and leg.

SUPERMAN

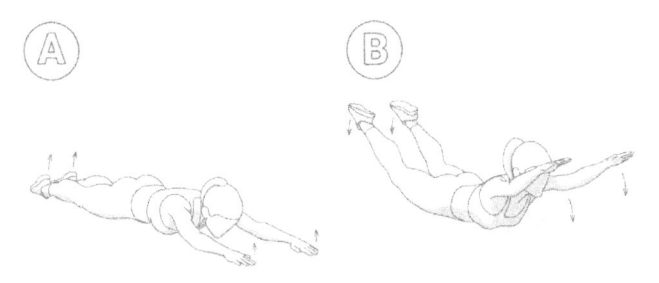

Ⓐ Ⓑ

Lat pulldowns

For this exercise, you will need a towel.

Stand with feet hip-width apart and a towel in your hands. Raise your arms straight above your head, slightly wider than your shoulders. Pull your arms away from each other, creating tension with the towel: this is your starting position.

Keeping this tension with the towel, lower your arms so the towel brushes your face, stop when the towel reaches shoulder height. Keeping the tension, raise your arms to start position. That's one repetition. Work towards 2 sets of 12 reps.

Grace Kelly arms

To create toned, shapely arms, we are going to use our body weight for resistance.

Tricep dips

With your hands facing forward, hip-distance apart, hold onto the edge of a bench or stable chair. With your legs extended out in front of you, lower your butt towards the floor, using just your arms. If this is too difficult with fully extended legs, bring your feet nearer to you while you build your strength. Build up gradually to reach 2 sets of 20 repetitions.

TRICEPS DIPS

Plank Jacks

This exercise works most of your body and is very good for toning arms and shoulders too. Start in a high plank position (on hands rather than elbows. Then, jump your feet in and out (like jumping jacks). This exercise is a good one to add to your HIIT routine.

PLANK JACKS

Strengthen your abs

No matter how strong your abs are, the fat needs to come off first – diet is key to see that toned core.

Below are some of the most effective abs exercises. I have not included crunches here. I think many people are bored with them, and it is one of the easiest to get wrong and put unnecessary pressure on your neck.

Dead bugs

This exercise is great for beginners and experts alike. It strengthens your whole core (the rectus abdominis, obliques, and transversus abdominis).

Lie on your back, arms and legs extended above you towards the ceiling, with legs bent at a 90-degree angle at the knees. With your back flat against the floor, make a conscious effort to keep your ribcage down: this is your starting position. Next, extend your left arm back towards the floor while at the same time straightening and lowering your right leg towards the floor. Bring back to the starting position. Repeat with the opposite arm and leg. That is one repetition. Work up towards 2 sets of 15 repetitions.

Only lower your arms and legs as far as they will go, without arching your back off the floor.

Bicycle

This exercise works all the core muscles, and it also helps tone your legs.

Lie on the floor; legs up, bent at the knee at 90 degrees, fingertips at the side of your head, head lifted off the floor, your back flat on the floor: this is your starting position. Then, contracting your abs, bring your right knee towards you, and at the same time rotate and lift your torso to touch your left elbow to this knee. Return to start. Repeat on the opposite arm and leg: this is one repetition. Work up to 2 sets of 20 repetitions.

Keep this exercise slow to help you keep your back flat to the floor throughout and work your core muscles effectively.

BICYCLE CRUNCH
WITH RESISTANCE BAND

Mountain climber

Mountain climbers work your whole body as well as core strength.

In a high plank position, pull your right knee up to your right elbow. Next, return your leg to starting position, and pull up your left knee to your left elbow. That's one rep. Build up to 2 sets of 30 repetitions. They are an excellent addition to your at-home HIIT routine. Speed it up if you are using it for HIIT, so it gets your heart pumping.

MOUNTAIN CLIMBERS

Ⓐ Ⓑ

Russian twists

The Russian twist is a great exercise to target the abdominals and obliques and can be modified to suit the beginner through to expert levels.

Sit on the floor, with your knees bent, heels on the floor. Lean back with your upper body, keeping your back straight.

For a beginner, link your fingers together, and keep your heels on the floor. From this position, twist your upper body from side to side.

For an intermediate level, lift your feet off the floor during this exercise.

For intermediate to advanced level, grab a weighted object, and hold this while you complete your reps.

Build up to 2 sets of 20 reps to each side.

RUSSIAN TWIST

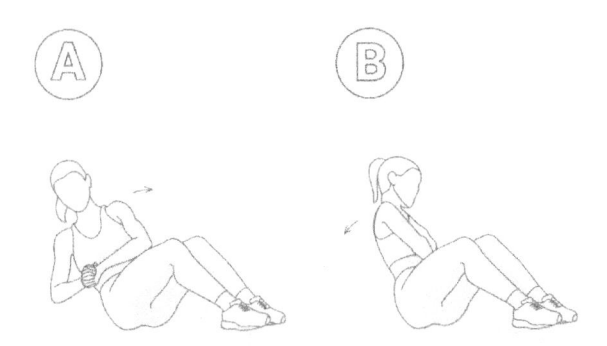

Stretch it all out

Chest

The doorframe stretch is a great way to correct rounded shoulders and is a great stretch if you've been sitting at a desk all day. It will help loosen up tight chest muscles, which pull our shoulders forward. Stand in a doorway, and place your forearms on the door frame, elbows just below shoulder level. Now gently lean forward, don't force the stretch. Hold for 20 seconds.

Hamstrings

Standing up, place one foot on a step, chair or bench. Both legs are straight. You may find placing your hands on your hips gives you more balance. Then, with your shoulders relaxed and keeping your back flat, hinge forward from your hips. Once you start to feel the stretch at the back of your thigh, stop, and hold for 1 – 2 minutes. Repeat on the other leg.

Quads

The quads are the major muscle at the front of your thigh.

To stretch this muscle, stand tall with your hand on a table or back of a chair for support. Now bend your right leg towards your butt, and grab hold of your ankle with your right hand. Keep standing nice and tall.

Pull your ankle gently further towards your butt until you feel a good stretch at the front of your thigh, but don't force the stretch, as it will put pressure on your knee. Hold for 45-60 seconds, and then swap legs.

QUADRICEPS STRETCH

STANDING VARIATION

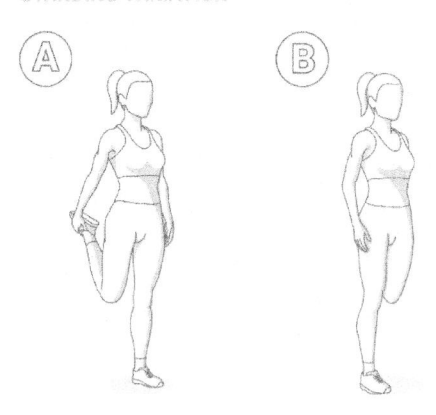

Calves

Tightness in the calf muscle can cause pain in your foot or knee.

The best stretch for calves is to stand on a step with the heel of one foot resting off the back of the step. Then, very gently, drop the heel down by bending the knee of your opposite leg. Hold for 30 seconds, then swap legs. Repeat a couple of times for each leg.

Hip flexors

The hip flexors could be one of the tightest muscles in our body. Our modern way of life, where we sit down for so many hours each day, is the root cause. This position shortens our hip flexors, leading to lower back pain and an excessively arched lower back (anterior pelvic tilt) as our body gets pulled out of balance.

To stretch this muscle out, kneel on your left knee, your right leg at a right angle in front of you. Your foot is flat on the floor with your knee in line with your heel. Now, two very subtle moves. First, tuck your tailbone under, and then lean forward ever so slightly. These are tiny movements. Once you feel a good stretch in your hip flexors, hold for 45 - 60 seconds, release, and swap legs.

Do this stretch every day if you have tight hip flexors or a tight lower back.

HIP FLEXOR STRETCH

Side stretch
Stretching out our torso is perfect first thing in the morning to help limber us up for the day.

Stand up with your feet hip-width apart. With your right arm down by your side, reach your left arm skywards, and without leaning backward or forwards, lean your upper body and left arm over to your right side. Hold for a few seconds, return to centre, and swap sides.

Yoga
Yoga is a great method of stretching, strengthening, and elongating your body and brings inner calmness. However, you don't need to become a full-blown 'yogi' to benefit from yoga.

Take a look online, and find a few poses you can incorporate into your daily routine. Just 5 mins a day will equal 30 hours of stretching over the course of a year!

Here are a few of my favourite yoga poses:
Warrior II Pose – a powerful pose to start your day with a focussed mind and strong body.
Tree Pose – this pose is great for balance and core stability.
The Cobbler's Pose – great for hip and inner thigh stretch.
Child's Pose – this pose relaxes the spine, shoulder, and neck and gently stretches out the lower back, hips, and thighs. A great way to wind down after a hectic day!

Creating your exercise plan

If you are new to exercise, you want to create a plan to challenge your body and change the way you look, but at the same time, give your body sufficient time to recover in between sessions.

Below is a suggestion on how to start if you are new to exercise. You can gradually add more sessions as your body becomes accustomed to exercise and gets stronger and fitter. Make sure you take at least one day of rest and recovery, no matter what level of fitness you have.

HIIT sessions: 20 – 30 minutes in total (including warm-up, cool down, and stretch).
Strength training: 30 – 50 minutes in total (including warm-up, cool down, and stretch).

Monday – strength training
Tuesday – HIIT
Wednesday – rest day
Thursday - strength training
Friday - – HIIT

Saturday – rest day
Sunday -– rest day

Starting out

1. **Start low and progress gradually**
   If you are new to exercise or haven't exercised in a while, start slowly and gradually progress to more reps and longer intervals as you improve your fitness level.

2. **Strengthen your entire body**
   Pick at least one exercise per body area from the strength and resistance section to exercise each muscle group. Then, either establish a set routine using these exercises or mix it up each time – whichever way works best for you.

3. **Focus on the muscle you are working**
   To help activate and exercise the correct muscle, focus on which muscle you are working. For example, with donkey kicks, instead of falling into the easy trap of slinging your leg up in the air – focus on lifting your leg using your glute (butt) muscles. Doing this will help you get the most benefit from each exercise. Some people find placing their hand on the actual muscle helps.

4. **Remember to warm up, cool down, and stretch out all muscles worked**
   Warming up can be as simple as having a good dance around your living room. Choose music that brings out your inner diva to get you in the perfect frame of mind. Warming up increases the blood flow to your muscles, raises your body

temperature slightly, and prepares your body for exercise.

Remember to cool down after exercise. If you are returning to your living room dance floor, choose something less energetic. Then stretch out the muscles you've worked to help them recover, and keep them long and supple. Refer to the 'Stretch it all out' section for some stretches you can do.

5. **Set yourself targets**

    Make these targets realistic, so they keep you motivated, but also challenging enough so that they also challenge you. Finally, take time to acknowledge and congratulate yourself when you have smashed through your targets – that's awesome! And then, set some new ones.

6. **Establish a routine**

    Schedule the same time of day, and same days of the week, for exercise. Then, block this time out in your diary. If you have a routine in place, it will be easier to establish exercise as a habit.

7. **Miss a session if you are not feeling well**

    If you are not feeling well, do not exercise – but do not miss a session because your favourite tv show is about to start!

8. **Monitor your progress**

    Keep an exercise diary and log how many repetitions you are doing. Take your body measurements so you can see how your body is changing. Take photos, because we easily forget how we used to look. Feel the difference in how your clothes fit and look on you. Again, take time to acknowledge and congratulate yourself on the progress you are making.

9. **Start, even when you don't feel like it**
By the time you have thought of enough excuses for why you aren't going to exercise, you could have almost finished your session and be one step nearer to your goal! While exercise is still new to you, it will take extra effort to pick yourself up and exercise. However, nothing is going to change if you stay on the sofa. Remember, you will get there. It just takes one step towards your goal, one day at a time.

Stepping it up a notch

This section works particularly well paired with the "Stepping it up a notch" section in Nutrition.

If you haven't already, now is a good time to invest in dumbbells, a barbell set, or even a gym membership.

While you can do the following exercises with weights at home, the gym will also offer an extensive range of machines.

At this stage, your body will have become used to a certain level of exercise. So, now we want to challenge your body to take it to the next level. A great way to do this is to add weights to the exercises we have already been doing. It will be the same for some exercises; for others, you will need to switch the form slightly.

Switch your routine up once you have been working out with a set routine for a couple of months. Switching your routine every 6- 8 weeks' will keep your body challenged and working in new ways. It will also make your workouts more enjoyable.

Weighted squats
As previously described, but this time adding weight. Hold a weight to your chest (to protect your back) or a barbell across the top of your shoulders. Be very careful when lifting the barbell onto your shoulders: brace your core to protect your back, and keep your back flat.
At the gym: try the leg press machine.

Weighted Lunges
As previously described, but we are now adding weight. Hold weight plates or dumbbells in both hands. Alternatively, a barbell across your shoulders; again, be careful when lifting the barbell up and onto your shoulders.

Chest press
The position is the same as the weighted floor press above. If you are using separate dumbbells, keep both arms at the same level throughout the exercise. Again, this is easier to manage using a barbell.
At the gym: Use the seated chest press or the cable machine for a more resistance-based workout.

Deadlift
This exercise is great for your back and hamstrings and also works your core. Start in a standing position, feet hip-width apart. Hold a barbell with an overhand grip (your palms facing the floor), slightly wider than shoulder-width apart. Keep a slight bend in your knees. Your feet should be flat on the floor, with the weight somewhat more in your heels.

Now, hinging from your hips, lower the bar towards the floor. Keep your back flat and the bar close to your thighs. Once you feel a stretch in your hamstrings, hold for 2 seconds, and then return to the starting position.

Romanian Deadlift

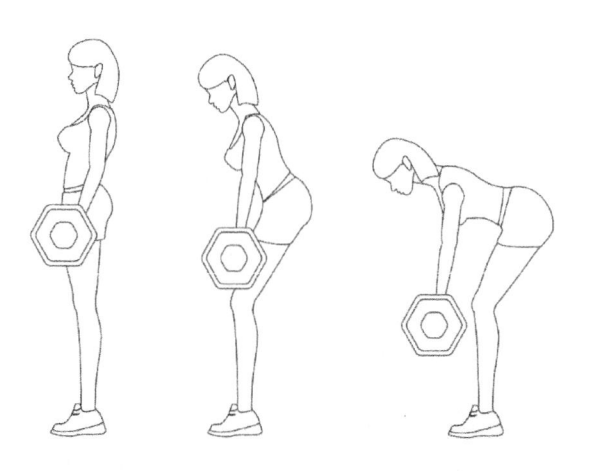

Dead row
Using the same movement as the deadlift, up until the point you have lowered the bar towards the floor. From this position, pull the bar in towards your belly button. Here, the only movement is from your arms. Keep your elbows pointing backward and not flaring out to the sides. Next, lower the bar back towards your knees, and then return to starting position. This exercise is great for your upper back and also works your core stability muscles.
At the gym: try the lat pulldown machine.

YOU
Getting across the finish line

The most important investment you will make in your life– is the investment in yourself.

This book aims to help you achieve your goal – losing weight, eating more healthily, or waking up feeling vibrant.

It will come as no surprise that the most common, top three New Year's Resolutions started with great enthusiasm are to: lose weight, exercise more, and eat more healthily.

Sadly, they are also the most commonly broken too.

So, whether it's procrastination, excuses, or waiting for the stars to align before you start, there's only one thing stopping you from getting where you are right now to where you want to be.

You.

So, how do we achieve what we so clearly desire?

Sometimes just having the right tools and information isn't enough to set us on our journey. Let me explain why.

Our <u>conscious</u> mind makes up 5% of our mind. We rely on this part of our brain to learn new things and do things differently.

Our <u>unconscious</u> mind makes up the remaining 95%. The unconscious mind is where our habits reside, along with all the thoughts of what we believe to be true. It's our personal blueprint.

Our blueprint automatically triggers most of our thoughts and actions without us even realising or being fully aware that they even exist. We rely on our blueprint to make all our decisions and create meaning out of life.

If what we are trying to achieve (conscious) isn't aligned with our blueprint (unconscious), we will struggle to implement the changes and achieve our desired results.

How is a personal blueprint created?
Your blueprint is created, mainly in your childhood, based on three elements:
1. Verbal – what you were told as a child

2. Modelling – these are the role models we learned from
3. Experience - these can be scenes from your life and situations you have been in, from which you have drawn a conclusion

From the moment we are born, we get filled with other people's thoughts, emotions, opinions, ways of doing things, and not doing something. These people include parents, family, caregivers, friends, and the media.

Is the information we are getting true or false? Neither. It's what they believe - or want us to believe - is true. If this is the case, you may wonder why this isn't obvious to all of us? Being surrounded by the people who gave us that way of thinking makes it feel normal.

80% of your brain's development comes before you reach the age of 3. We are too young to distinguish between what is factual and what is merely someone's opinion. Therefore, we absorb like sponges, and we take all we hear onboard as fact. And it gets saved onto our mental hard drive.

By the time we are old enough to distinguish between fact and opinion, these beliefs are already hard-wired into our blueprint and trigger us automatically, without us even realising or being fully aware that they even exist.

It's not who you are - it's who you learned to be.

And it is your <u>blueprint</u> that <u>determines your results</u>.

So, how does your blueprint affect your results?
Put very simply; it's a chain reaction:

Our mental programming creates our THOUGHTS, which in turn creates our FEELINGS, leading to the ACTIONS we take, which determines the RESULTS we achieve.

Let's look at a couple of examples of blueprints in action.

You may have heard of Roger Bannister, who, back in 1954, broke through the four-minute mile barrier in 3 minutes 59 seconds.

What you may not know was up until that point, most people thought trying to run this fast would cause the body to self-combust! Although records show from 1886, some runners had been on a quest to break this barrier; it was still considered impossible. So that's at least <u>68 years</u> of trying before Bannister achieved it.

<u>Forty-six days</u> after Bannister broke the record, guess what happened? Someone smashed the world record he set! This time at 3 minutes 58 seconds. And since then, more than a thousand runners have run a mile in under 4 minutes.

How was that so? Was there a sudden evolution in human capabilities? Was there a discovery in genetic engineering? Did we suddenly give birth to a new breed of super runners?

No. What changed was the mental model.

The past runners were held back by a belief that breaking the four-minute mile barrier was impossible. However, once <u>one</u> man broke it, it suddenly became possible for <u>everyone</u>.

Before we turn our attention to you, there are a couple of other examples to think about because understanding how this works is important.

Statistics have shown 70% of lottery winners who were broke pre-win go back to being broke within a few years? Why? Because they do not possess the mental blueprint to deal with financial abundance.

This model also works the other way: how many millionaires have you heard of who have lost their entire fortune, only to recoup it back again – sometimes more than once! George Foreman and Walt Disney are two examples. Their unconscious blueprint is one of success and wealth.

What if you don't like your blueprint? What if you want different results?

Well, here's the good news - we can change our blueprint!

We saw above how our mental programming creates our THOUGHTS, which in turn creates our FEELINGS, leading to the ACTIONS we take, which determines the RESULTS we achieve.

Changing your blueprint comes down to 3 simple steps – and I'm betting there has already been a time in your life where you have taken these three steps.

Let's take a look.

Think of a big win or accomplishment in your life that at one time was a dream or a goal that seemed impossible for you to achieve. Something that, when you look back on, makes you feel ever so proud. Perhaps this was career-related or financial. Maybe a relationship or a fitness goal?

Now take a few moments and transport yourself back to that time. What did you do to cause this accomplishment? Think of your attitude, any actions you took, your determination and focus, and anything else that springs to mind.

In answering these questions, you may have come up with some, or all, of the following:
1. You decided this is for me. You focused on it. You got obsessed.
2. Your desire for this goal was so strong that it unleashed the energy that drove you to find the answers to achieve it.
3. You took action. You didn't let anything get in your way of achieving that dream or goal.

Now, we need to create that same focus, energy, and momentum for your goal that brought you here to this book.

Step 1 – get a big enough 'why' for this goal

Having a big enough 'why' for this goal will get you focused and obsessed to achieve it. We are going to use the concept of a mind map for this step, as follows:

On a large sheet of paper – A4 size or bigger, write down your goal in the middle of the page. For example, it might be to lose weight, eat healthier, or gain more energy. Whatever it was that made you pick up this book.

Now draw some lines outwards from that central goal. At the end of each line, write down one reason for wanting this goal or one outcome that you will achieve on reaching your goal.

Some things to include to get you started: How does it feel? What do you look like? How are friends and family reacting? How will it impact other areas of your life – relationships, confidence, sports, hobbies? What clothes are you wearing? How do you stand when looking at your reflection in the mirror? What is it about it that *really* excites you?

Using coloured pens for this exercise makes it more visually appealing.
When you have completed it, stick it somewhere where you can see it every day. Then, you can continue to add new outcomes to the mind map as they spring to mind.

How to use your mind map
Have you ever seen two teams playing a sport, where one team is completely dominating the first half, the other team trailing behind, looking and feeling defeated? Then the whistle goes off at half-time. The teams go off, and when they return, something has changed. The team that had looked defeated is now fired up. Their hunger re-ignited. They are suddenly standing taller and stronger, dominating the second half of this game. We've all seen it, right?
That must have been some half-time pep-talk!

When you get knocked off-kilter, feel like throwing in the towel, or simply having an off day, this mind map is the equivalent of that pep-talk at half-time - this will remind you of the purpose and reignite the energy for why you are doing this.

Step 2 – the importance of being 'all in'
So, what do I mean here by being 'all in'? Do this with everything you've got.
Don't go into this half committed, one foot in and one foot out. There's no dabbling or giving this a 'try.'

To use another sports analogy. We've all seen a player in some sport going to kick or shoot a ball. When you've watched them, you've thought to yourself, "They are going to miss it." And what happens? They miss it. What was it that made you think they were going to miss it? A slight hesitation, their posture, the way they moved? Whatever it was, there was that moment of uncertainty that the player had that you picked up on.

When you feel uncertain, or unsure, or worry that you might fail, you hold back from using your full potential – on being all in. So, the actions you take are hesitant and weaker, which gives you small, weak results.
And this can quickly spiral downwards.

You decide to try again, but now you are harbouring even more uncertainty because you didn't get the results you wanted the last time. So, the action you take now is even less committed. And then, what do you say about the results you fail to achieve? "See, I told you it wouldn't work," "I told you it wouldn't happen/would be a waste of time/wasn't for me."

Sound familiar?

Let's get that spiral moving upwards.

So, if feeling uncertain holds us back from using our full potential, how do we create more certainty in ourselves?

As we've seen above, just trying over and over again doesn't necessarily lead us to success. Perhaps you've had that experience with trying to lose weight before?

OK, time for a quick, fun exercise. If you cannot do this right now, please make sure you come back and do it when you can.

Stand up with your arms by your side. Now lift your right arm straight in front of you, and point ahead with your right index finger.

Without moving your feet, turn your upper body to the right, continue as far around as you comfortably can, and without losing your balance. Note the position of where your finger is pointing. Good. Come back to face forwards, and drop your right arm back to your side.

Now, close your eyes and visualize yourself doing this same exercise without lifting your arm and moving your body. Then, again, visualise yourself doing this. This time, as you turn, you see yourself going round much, much further, and you do it with such ease. Then, in your mind, bring yourself back to face forward again.

Do this again. Just in your mind, your arm is raised, and you are turning around. This time you see yourself turning even further than the last time, and it is so easy to do! Bring yourself back to face forward again.

Now, repeat this process one last time. This time, in your mind, you see yourself spinning around so much further than before. You've almost turned a full circle! It's enjoyable and easy to do. Bring yourself back to face forward again.

Now, open your eyes. Lift your right arm straight in front of you as before, pointing with your right index finger. Turn around as far as you comfortably can. What happened? Did you go round much further than the first time? I imagine so. How much further? If you are like 80% of the people that do this, you will have turned 25% further than on your first attempt! Crazy, right? Why is this so? We hadn't physically changed anything to our bodies in that time.

But we did change our beliefs.

In our mind, we saw ourselves going further, and that was with just three quick visualisations.

The power of our mind is incredible.

Where were we before we did this exercise?
I had asked if feeling uncertain holds us back from using our full potential; how do we create more certainty of ourselves?

Now you have the answer: we **visualise it first.**

When you set yourself goals or targets, see a vision of you achieving them in your mind. Scientific studies have shown that the same brain region is stimulated in the same way, regardless of whether an action is visualised, or carried out. That means our brain cannot tell the difference between reality and our visualisations. Visualisation is so effective that actors, speakers, and sportspeople successfully use this technique to prepare for their upcoming performances.

We don't need to spend hours doing this. But if our thoughts create our reality, why not use these thoughts to set ourselves up for success, rather than choose thoughts that lower our confidence and diminish our chances of achieving our goals?

You can see for yourself in the short exercise above how it worked for you.

Now go back to your mind map from Step 1, and visualise all the outcomes you had written down as vividly as you can in your mind. Do this every day.

Step 3 – create momentum

The third, and final step, is creating positive momentum. How do we do this?

With our newfound certainty, we tap into our full potential. Tapping into our whole potential means when we take action, we create better results. As we develop better results, our confidence and belief in ourselves expand. As our beliefs grow, we have more certainty, and this is how we create a positive cycle of upward momentum. Exactly where we want to be.

But we must take action.

There is a saying - knowledge is power. However, knowing and not using it doesn't make you powerful. It's acting upon that knowledge, putting it to use, that creates the power.

Having and accomplishing something you don't have right now comes down to your ability to do something you aren't doing now. Taking action can be uncomfortable, but staying comfortable is not good. Comfortable is where you are now. Comfortable is familiar.

Becoming a better version of yourself will be uncomfortable – at first. However, repetition makes it a lot easier, and over time, that repetition becomes a habit. All of a sudden, you are the 'new you' without even thinking about it.

Think about when you were first learning to drive. All those things you had to do – all at the same time! What?! Change gears, look in the mirror, hands on the steering wheel, keep your eye on the road and the traffic signals, and the driver in front of you – all at the same time - are you kidding!!

How easily and naturally does that come to you now? Sometimes we drive from A to B and don't even recall the journey!

Things are more challenging when learning because it is more of a conscious effort to do these new things. However, with practice and repetition, the actions become more natural to us, they sink into our subconscious, and those actions then become effortless.

Action is critical.

Starting out

1. Identify the actions that will take you from where you are now to where you want to be.
2. Which of the actions identified will have the most significant impact? Focus on the top 2 or 3.
3. Identify what incremental change you can implement today. Why incremental? An incremental shift over time will have huge effects, but the effort won't feel so great. This means you are

more likely to stick to these gradual changes, making them a habit faster and building your confidence to make more incremental changes.
4. Schedule when you will commit and what you will commit to.
5. What will be the likely blockers or challenges to you achieving your goal? Imagine these challenges happening, and now imagine your response to them which will keep you on track. Did that response work? Yes? Fantastic. No, or did other challenges come up? Then find responses to those too. Practice and practice visualising your responses. So, when the challenge actually happens (which, of course, it will!) you will automatically know how to respond to it – because you have rehearsed the scenario in advance.
6. Take action towards your goal every day. Regular action reinforces the habit.
7. At the start of each day: before your feet have even touched the floor, begin with the right frame of mind. Visualise all the outcomes you had written down on your mind map above. How good does that success feel? Today you are going to take more action! Recall the steps you took the previous day (no matter how small!), and give yourself a high five!
8. At the end of each day: as your head hits the pillow, congratulate yourself for actions you took towards your goal. It is important to go to sleep feeling good. Your subconscious does not sleep when you do, so we want to feed it good thoughts to chew on overnight.
9. Focus on where you are going, not where you have been or where you are coming from. Remember, it's not where you start; it's where you go.

10. Don't wait for the right moment or 'the perfect time'. We are never ready - we become ready.
11. All action is positive. It either takes you in the right direction – great if it does, or it gives you the information you need to adjust. Either way, it is <u>forward motion</u>.
12. Look at what you will be gaining instead of what you think you will be missing. For example, instead of thinking of this as a 'diet', think of it as a plan of action to help you achieve a healthier body/more vitality/a spring in your step/greater confidence.
13. If you feel overwhelmed, break your actions down into smaller achievable steps, and take each step, one at a time.
14. Remember, with each action you take, you weaken the old wiring and simultaneously build and strengthen new neural pathways – a new blueprint. A new you.

This chapter provides you with the 3-step process to adopt the success mindset to achieve your goal. For any of you still sat on the fence about doing these exercises, a little nudge, if I may. What got you here won't get you there, and if you don't make the changes now, how will your life and body be different this time next year?

Insanity is doing the same thing over and over again and expecting different results - Albert Einstein

Some of you may be wondering what other ceilings your blueprint has set for you.

If you would like to explore your blueprint further and change it to achieve more significant results, please drop me an email at:
coaching@quantumleapmylife.com

Recap of the three steps to success:
In **Step 1**, we created your mind map. Use this as a reminder of the big 'why' for your goal: this will keep you focused and obsessed to want to achieve it.

When you get knocked off-kilter or are simply having an off day - which we all do, life happens - this mind map is the equivalent of the pep-talk you give yourself at half-time. Your mind map will remind you of the purpose and reignite the energy for why you are doing this.

In **Step 2**, we covered the importance of being 'all in'. Then, we saw how when we act with uncertainty, we get mediocre results. Finally, we did an exercise to demonstrate how our mind can hold us back without being aware of it – and how we can use visualisation to change that.

In **Step 3**, we talked about creating positive upward momentum towards achieving your goal. We discussed how staying comfortable was going to keep you exactly where you are now. We talked about taking uncomfortable action to become an even better version of yourself, and how with repetition, new behaviours become effortless habits.

Put these three simple steps into practice, and you will see the results before you know it!

Discipline isn't on your back needling you with imperatives; it's at your side encouraging you with incentives
- Sybil Stanton

CLOSING WORDS

Thank you for buying my book. I hope you have enjoyed it, at least half as much as I have enjoyed writing it.
Better still, I hope you are well on your way to achieving the body you truly want and deserve. Let's face it, we all deserve to look and feel our best without sacrificing all the pleasures life has to offer.

I tried to balance the book between providing you with enough scientific detail (and not an encyclopaedia) and giving you a concise tool, so you can get on with becoming leaner, stronger, and healthier.

In doing so, I may have missed something you need. If you have any questions as you implement the steps, I would like to help. You can email me at susan@quantumleapmylife.com I answer all emails personally.

If you would like more support with implementing any of the steps in the book, there is an online course, and I offer group and 1:1 coaching. For more information on these options, please drop me an email at coaching@quantumleapmylife.com

The real joy for me will be knowing I have helped someone look and feel better than they have ever done before. I would love to hear how you have got on. I read all feedback and reviews. Also, by leaving feedback for this book, you may help someone else make the same journey you have.

I wish you and your new body all the very best!

Susan

REFERENCES

1. Fothergill E, Guo J, Howard L, Kerns JC, Knuth ND, Brychta R, Chen KY, Skarulis MC, Walter M, Walter PJ, Hall KD. Persistent metabolic adaptation 6 years after "The Biggest Loser" competition. Obesity (Silver Spring). 2016 Aug;24(8):1612-9. doi: 10.1002/oby.21538. Epub 2016 May 2. PMID: 27136388; PMCID: PMC4989512.
2. De Vriese C, Delporte C. Influence of ghrelin on food intake and energy homeostasis. Curr Opin Clin Nutr Metab Care. 2007 Sep;10(5):615-9. doi: 10.1097/MCO.0b013e32829fb37c. PMID: 17693746.
3. Epel ES, McEwen B, Seeman T, Matthews K, Castellazzo G, Brownell KD, Bell J, Ickovics JR. Stress and body shape: stress-induced cortisol secretion is consistently greater among women with central fat. Psychosom Med. 2000 Sep-Oct;62(5):623-32. doi: 10.1097/00006842-200009000-00005. PMID: 11020091.
4. Zauner C, Schneeweiss B, Kranz A, Madl C, Ratheiser K, Kramer L, Roth E, Schneider B, Lenz K. Resting energy expenditure in short-term starvation is increased as a

result of an increase in serum norepinephrine. Am J Clin Nutr. 2000 Jun;71(6):1511-5. doi: 10.1093/ajcn/71.6.1511. PMID: 10837292.
5. Boden G, Sargrad K, Homko C, Mozzoli M, Stein TP. Effect of a low-carbohydrate diet on appetite, blood glucose levels, and insulin resistance in obese patients with type 2 diabetes. Ann Intern Med. 2005 Mar 15;142(6):403-11. doi: 10.7326/0003-4819-142-6-200503150-00006. PMID: 15767618.
6. Stockman MC, Thomas D, Burke J, Apovian CM. Intermittent Fasting: Is the Wait Worth the Weight? *Curr Obes Rep.* 2018;7(2):172-185. doi:10.1007/s13679-018-0308-9
7. Longo VD, Mattson MP. Fasting: molecular mechanisms and clinical applications. *Cell Metab.* 2014;19(2):181-192. doi:10.1016/j.cmet.2013.12.008
8. Takaya J, Higashino H, Kobayashi Y. Intracellular magnesium and insulin resistance. Magnes Res. 2004 Jun;17(2):126-36. PMID: 15319146. Takaya J, Higashino H, Kobayashi Y. Intracellular magnesium and insulin resistance. Magnes Res. 2004 Jun;17(2):126-36. PMID: 15319146.
9. Boirie Y, Dangin M, Gachon P, Vasson MP, Maubois JL, Beaufrère B. Slow and fast dietary proteins differently modulate postprandial protein accretion. Proc Natl Acad Sci U S A. 1997 Dec 23;94(26):14930-5. doi: 10.1073/pnas.94.26.14930. PMID: 9405716; PMCID: PMC25140.
10. Arnal MA, Mosoni L, Boirie Y, Houlier ML, Morin L, Verdier E, Ritz P, Antoine JM, Prugnaud J, Beaufrère B, Mirand PP. Protein feeding pattern does not affect protein retention in young women. J Nutr. 2000 Jul;130(7):1700-4. doi: 10.1093/jn/130.7.1700. PMID: 10867039.
11. LaForgia J, Withers RT, Gore CJ. Effects of exercise intensity and duration on the excess post-exercise oxygen consumption. J Sports Sci. 2006 Dec;24(12):1247-64. doi: 10.1080/02640410600552064. PMID: 17101527.
12. Almuzaini, K.S., Potteiger, J.A., and Green, S.B. 1998. Effects of split exercise sessions on excess post-exercise oxygen consumption and resting metabolic rate. Canadian Journal of Applied Physiology, 23(5), 433-443

13. Townsend LK, Couture KM, Hazell TJ. Mode of exercise and sex are not important for oxygen consumption during and in recovery from sprint interval training. Appl Physiol Nutr Metab. 2014 Dec;39(12):1388-94. doi: 10.1139/apnm-2014-0145. PMID: 25386979.
14. Volek JS, Noakes T, Phinney SD. Rethinking fat as a fuel for endurance exercise. Eur J Sport Sci. 2015;15(1):13-20. doi: 10.1080/17461391.2014.959564. Epub 2014 Oct 2. PMID: 25275931.

Printed in Great Britain
by Amazon